THE NAKED FEET OF NICARAGUA

The Naked Feet
of Nicaragua

Nick Cole and Dennis Smith

Hodder & Stoughton
LONDON SYDNEY AUCKLAND

British Library Cataloguing in Publication Data
A record for this book is available from the British Library

ISBN 0 340 64303 X
ISBN 0 340 66929 2

Typeset by Hewer Text Composition Services, Edinburgh
Printed and bound in Great Britain by
Mackays, Chatham, Kent

Hodder and Stoughton Ltd
A Division of Hodder Headline PLC
338 Euston Road
London NW1 3BH

Contents

Foreword

As the Ambassador to the Court of St James, but most of all as a Nicaraguan citizen, I am grateful to Nick Cole and Dennis Smith for writing this book. *The Naked Feet of Nicaragua* shows the selfless commitment and caring nature of an amazing group of young and not-so-young Britons who, driven by their Christian beliefs and their desire to give 'a little sunshine of God's love', brought hope and care to the less fortunate in my country.

The contagious enthusiasm, deeply rooted conviction and Christian vision of the team leader, Michael Cole, assured the success of this 'adventure with a purpose'.

This book gives a fascinating account of the historic developments in the eastern coast of Nicaragua, the Mosquito Shore. From the brief incursion of young Lord Nelson to the hectic days of the California Gold Rush, the San Juan river was considered to be the favoured route to connect the two great seas.

In 1995, 'the English came back to the river San Juan'. *The Naked Feet of Nicaragua* depicts the story of this project which, combined with the human drive and technological innovation of the hovercraft, made the remote area of the Mosquito Shore more accessible to the rest of the country; more important, it established a true link 'through the oceans' by creating a brotherhood between these two peoples. This time, the English not only came in peace, but they managed to improve and light up the lives and destinies of the thousands of people whom their efforts reached.

Verónica Lacayo de Gómez
Ambassador of Nicaragua

Acknowledgments

It was gracious of **doña Violeta Barrios de Chamorro,** in the midst of her heavy schedule as President of the Nicaraguan Republic, to send us the material from which we took our title, and not a little of our inspiration.

From **John Culver,** Her Majesty's Ambassador to Nicaragua, and from his wife, **Margaret,** we have received throughout advice, support and genuine friendship.

We are grateful to **doña Verónica Lacayo de Gómez,** Nicaraguan Ambassador in London, who has been generous in many ways, especially in helping our understanding of the complexities of recent Nicaraguan history.

We thank **Mike Cole** for the inspiration his vision and enthusiasm engender, which makes projects like this – and books about them – possible.

We thank those nearest to us, our wives **Jenny** and **Brenda,** who read our manuscripts and helped us the better to know how you, our readers, were likely to understand what we had written.

We appreciated the practical support given by **Colin** and **Sue Winter** in the loan of an excellent personal computer.

Where we have quoted from other people's work we have tried to give due credit. If, inadvertently, we have been in any way unfair we hope to be forgiven for Nicaragua's sake.

We acknowledge your kindness in buying or borrowing our book. If there should be any who feel they have been asked to pay too high a price for owning a copy, we can only offer the consolation that every pound of royalties and profits is being given to the BRITISH HOVERCRAFT PROJECT TO NICARAGUA, 1995–1998, and so thank you for sharing in our commitment to the isolated Nicaraguan people.

Lastly, we are grateful to each other, for the trust we have been able to place in one another as we have painted the scene from our different perspectives, expressed convictions in our different styles, yet met our deadlines with identical determination.

NICK COLE   DENNIS SMITH

The British Hovercraft Project to Nicaragua 1995 - 1998

- - - Hovercraft Journey 1995 – El Rama to Old Leon

HONDURAS

NICARAGUA

Puerto Cabezas

Estelí

Corinto

CARIBBEAN SEA

PEARL LAGOON

Bluefields

Rio Grande

El Rama

Rio Escondido

Monkey Point

Nueva Guinea

Rio Punta Gorda

Greytown
(San Juan
del Norte)

Rio Indio

El Castillo

Rio San Juan

San Carlos

Juigalpa

San Pancho

COSTA RICA

Rio Tipitapa

Las Isletas

Solentiname

LAKE NICARAGUA

Ometepe Island

Momotombo

LAKE MANAGUA

Tipitapa

Granada

Old León

MANAGUA

Rívas

San Juan del Sur

PACIFIC OCEAN

COLUMBIA

MEXICO

GUATEMALA

BELIZE

EL SALVADOR

HONDURAS

NICARAGUA

COSTA RICA

PANAMA

COLUMBIA

Prologue

Nicaragua is a country in need. Her history, since the birth of the Republic, has been as volcanic as her geography. Periods of peace and progress have been very much the exception.

Sadly, she has often found herself a pawn in somebody else's boardgame. First it was the struggle between the European powers for a New World empire; then the determination of North American settlers to extend their frontiers to the west against all odds.

More recently Nicaragua has found herself involved in the ideological struggle between, on the one hand, the communist bloc's Cuba-led support of the Sandinista revolution and, on the other, the determination of the United States that nothing like that was going to happen in their backyard! Hence their support of the *Contras* and the Irangate scandal. But the civil war was no 'game' for Nicaragua. It decimated her population, left her countryside ravaged, her surviving people divided but with a deep-seated yearning for a lasting peace.

Human beings have been unkind to Nicaragua, but the so-called 'acts of God' have brought their suffering too. Earthquakes have flattened her cities, hurricanes and tidal waves her coastline. Diseases threaten: typhoid, cholera, malaria and dengue fever. Together, these disasters had brought the Nicaraguan economy to the very edge – many would say over the edge – of disaster.

A few years of fragile democracy have produced a measure of peace, but as yet no measure of prosperity. But she need not be this poor. 'We are beggars squatting in paradise,' is the considered opinion of Dr Jaime Incer, a renowned Nicaraguan geographer.

The situation is seriously compounded by international debt. Nicaragua owes US$11 billion to the world's bankers. Think of that in terms of individuals. There are four million Nicaraguans to share the burden of that debt, which works out at over US$2,500 per Nicaraguan man, woman and child. The Gross National Product in per capita terms is $430 per annum. So the 'average Nicaraguan' enjoys an income of $430 a year with which to repay a debt of $2,500. Unless something extraordinary is arranged by her creditors the country will remain poor for years to come.

Nicaragua, undeniably, is a country in need.

*   *   *   *   *

Was there nothing we could do?

Until quite recently, young people who wanted to serve Christ overseas approached it as a vocation, a call of God to a life's work. After obligatory studies, they joined a Christian Mission, spent a year or two in language and cultural adaptation, and then worked in their chosen field until retirement. We used to call them 'missionaries'.

During the past twenty years a new breed has emerged, Christian volunteers with energies and talents to offer to a given situation for a given period of time. TV has penetrated the comfort of our homes with the graphic portrayal of Third World poverty, and some have been moved enough to go and do something about it.

Why society should have chosen to lampoon them as 'do-gooders', when there are so many loutish and drug-ridden elements around on which it could unload its deprecation, is a question that only society itself can answer.

It has not always been easy to slot this new breed of activity into the traditional patterns. Protests, marked by more than a touch of cynicism, have not been uncommon: 'What can you hope to achieve in a few weeks – or six months for that matter

– without even the language? And who's going to pick up the tab when you go back home?' Serious questions. Happily the benefits have so greatly outweighed any disruption caused to established programmes that the clock could never be turned back. Short-term volunteers have come to stay, and have a clear part to play in taking the love of Christ across cultures.

Latin Link is a mission which has now run over a hundred and fifty different short-term projects, in half a dozen Latin American countries, involving more than 2000 young people. Aid has been taken to refugees, flood victims, orphanages and centres for 'street children'; classrooms have been constructed for schools, dormitories for Bible schools, and other buildings for community centres, clinics and churches. Latin leaders have been voluble – and still are – in their praise and appreciation of all that is being done.

But the constructions are not the only – perhaps not even the most important – benefit to be left behind. The sight of a team of young men and women from well-to-do European families toiling unpaid, on behalf of a people they have never met before, sweat-soaked, dust-covered and mud-caked, has left many Latin Americans standing in astonished disbelief. What would they say if they knew that volunteers actually pay for the privilege of going?

Most young Latins who go to university are strictly disinclined to tackle dirty-hand jobs; such work is the unfortunate lot of those less well-equipped to avoid it! That manual labour might be a part of Christian servanthood and dignify in some way the one who labours is, in general, a concept far removed from Latin American thought. Disciplined short-term volunteers have probably done more to bridge that cultural gap than anything since the *Discovery*!

Perhaps our young people are being driven, in some measure, by a sense of guilt, inheriting as they do comforts and privileges denied to so many. A war correspondent who had been felled by a shell-burst in the Far East, and broke an arm when blown off a roof filming in El Salvador, turned up later on *Desert Island Discs* and was asked if the dangers of the job ever tempted him to give up. 'Not really,' he said.

'I think I would find it totally unacceptable to go on filming the pain and the blood while remaining comfortably ignorant of what it actually feels like to ache and to bleed. To share in some way the suffering I am meant to record seems to me an indispensable qualification for doing my job well.'

If that is true for a cameraman, how much more for a Christian whose Gospel claims to have an answer to human need. So when we ask our returning volunteers if they have any regrets about the price paid or the pain experienced, most will undoubtedly echo the correspondent and say: 'No. I think I would have found it unacceptable to go on every year moved by the poverty of the TV documentaries while remaining comfortably ignorant of what it actually feels like to be poor. To share in some way the suffering that has moved me seems an indispensable qualification for being a true Christian in today's unequal world.'

*   *   *   *   *

Retired Squadron Leader Michael Cole, OBE, was appointed Director of Latin Link's short-term programme in the mid-eighties. He found, in his seemingly limitless pool of volunteers, the human resources to make a worthwhile contribution to Nicaragua. But there then appeared another element which turned a simple willingness to help into a technical and financial challenge of a much higher order.

In its short article on HOVERCRAFT, a popular encyclopaedia has the following: *Best adapted to use on lakes, sheltered coastal waters, river estuaries and swamps, and places where harbours have not been established.* Add a few rapids, shallows and sandbars, and you have a perfectly adequate description of the Caribbean coast, one of the most isolated and abandoned parts of Nicaragua. Which must be why the British Ambassador encouraged Mike, when developing his short-term projects in Nicaragua, to think of taking a hovercraft, as well as his volunteers, to that particular area of the country.

Throw a gauntlet of that description at the feet of a man like Mike Cole and you must not expect him to leave it lying there. He picked it up, and this book is about what happened next.

Chapter 1

Linking Oceans

A river lies at the heart of this story – the river San Juan in the south-east corner of Nicaragua. It is a river largely unknown, untravelled and unappreciated. But it ought not to be so, for there was a time when it brought Nicaragua firmly to the centre of the world's attention.

The Spaniards discovered in the 16th century that the river San Juan drained Nicaragua's great inland sea to the Atlantic Ocean, and that it created – save for a few short miles – a path of water between the great oceans. Yet they left the river strangely neglected, its potential painfully untapped.

Then, in 1849, something happened that was to change all that. A carpenter from New York saw gold glitter at the bottom of a stream in California. North American settlers had for long been pushing their frontiers westwards, only the hazards of the prairie keeping many at home. But now, hazards notwithstanding, getting to California became an imperative for tens of thousands. The gold rush had begun.

There were three ways of reaching San Francisco from New York. You could take your covered waggon west, buy a ticket for the long sea voyage round Cape Horn, or take an intermediate route part by sea and part by land across the Central American isthmus. The open prairie was by far the shortest and may well seem today to have been the obvious choice, though a comfortable seat in a modern cinema to watch a 'western' is not the best of places from which to discern the probable cost of such a journey. Of the three thousand or more

1

miles to California, not less than two-thirds involved crossing bone-rattling trails which were far from clearly marked. The possibility of losing your way, your animals, your waggons – or even your scalp – was certainly a very real one.

The journey round the New World's southernmost tip, however, was ten thousand miles longer, took three months or more, and entailed passing through the infamously stormy straits of Magellan. It was none the less the route taken by thousands of goldrushers, including Europeans, most of whom came from Germany, France or the British Isles.[1]

The third route appeared to have much going for it. Crossing the Panamanian jungle on foot saved some 8,000 miles off the trip round the Horn, and entailed very few miles over unknown territory. Furthermore, it was cheaper! Much depended on what time of the year you chose to travel. When the weather was kind and the mosquitoes in some abeyance, the trip could apparently prove an enjoyable experience. But at other times, survivors emerged from the Darien rain forest caked in Panamanian mud, hollow-eyed, ravenously hungry and, more often than not, sick with any one of a number of life-threatening diseases.

The choice cannot have been an easy one, and some horrors were common to all options. Cholera was rife up and down the prairie caravans, and the newly blazed trails were soon rather more readily identifiable by the string of freshly dug graves along the way. The trip indeed was so appalling that very few of those who had made their fortunes or – which was far more likely – had been driven to return home disillusioned and empty-handed, ever contemplated returning by land. Almost without exception they sailed south to cross the isthmus.

But cholera was no more merciful there. One ship heading south from San Francisco buried thirty-seven at sea before reaching Panama City.[2] Travellers were getting blasé about malaria. You took your chances; the rigors usually subsided anyway! But yellow fever could not be accepted as a fact of life in quite the same way, and by 1850 it had instilled fear into seafarers the world over. If you fell victim in Panama, your chances of survival were no more than fifty-fifty. Even if you yourself escaped, watching travelling companions die would have been horrendous. Uncontrollable shivering, high fever and raging thirst were accompanied by excruciating head and back pains. If followed by the dreaded 'black vomit' stage, a catastrophic drop in body temperature ensued which invariably proved fatal. Little wonder therefore that one prospector wrote home from the Panamanian swamps to those thinking of following him: 'I say, in fear of God and love of man . . . on no consideration come this route. I have nothing to say for the other routes, but do not take this one.'[3]

None the less, lured by El Dorado, thousands went on spurning death and disease to get to California. Then someone was heard describing Nicaragua as a country of friendly people and peaceful rivers, where cattle grazed on fertile plains backed by panoramic volcanoes, and the oceans were no more than 150 miles apart. Thus Nicaragua became accepted increasingly as an alternative route across the isthmus. In 1853 a total of some twenty thousand prospectors chose to travel it.

The isthmus was crossed in a sort of 'hop, skip and jump'. Very soon a North American entrepreneur had founded the Cornelius Vanderbilt Transport Company to enable you to do so 'in comfort'. In New York or Washington you bought a ticket for San Francisco, and sailed south to Greytown, at the mouth of the San Juan river. Since this was a British protectorate at the time, you could still speak English there – a not inconsiderable advantage. The 'hop' took you a few days up the river through the rain forest by canoe or in a specially designed flat-bottomed boat. You then 'skipped' across Lake Nicaragua in a reasonably comfortable steamer, and finally 'jumped' into a stage coach for the last twenty miles or so to the Pacific, over a road which was, for its day, remarkably well laid.

The playful simile should not be misinterpreted. The journey in general would still have been a formidable undertaking! But the new route was five hundred miles shorter, and got you to California several days sooner than going via Panama, and with quite a few more dollars left in your pocket.

But then the construction of a railway got under way

further south, and by the middle of the decade locomotives were steaming through the parrot-filled jungles of Panama carrying US mail, as well as prospectors. Shares in the Panama Railroad Company soared on the New York Stock Exchange, and fortunes were made by people who had never seen a Californian nugget or a bag of gold dust.

But the inter-oceanic possibilities offered by the San Juan in Nicaragua had been demonstrated to the world, and when some years later trading nations began thinking seriously of a canal, it was fresh in the world's memory and continued to give Nicaragua a centrality in international affairs out of all proportion to her size or wealth. Europe had begun to enjoy the enormous benefits of the canal at Suez, and the world now knew the benefits to be had by linking oceans. Nicaragua became to the New World what Egypt had been to the Old.

There were soon very serious plans afoot to cut a canal through to the Pacific. The debate – in which understandably the United States played a major role – centred on the most suitable siting for such an enterprise. Five possible routes were reviewed; three crossed what is today the Republic of Panama, one Nicaragua and the other Mexico. This last was early discarded but, until 1901, Nicaragua remained the site most likely to be chosen.

Before the end of the century an abortive attempt was in fact made to cut a few miles at the mouth of the San Juan river, a project which strangely failed to evoke much support from the Nicaraguan Presidency. The rusting hulk of an enormous dredge can still be seen at the entrance to the river. The long discussion about the most suitable site culminated in 1902 in a fourteen-day debate in the US Senate. When the talking started Nicaragua was the likely favourite but, after a fortnight of frantic lobbying, the result went the other way, with forty-two for Panama and thirty-four for Nicaragua.

Perhaps the most influential argument against Nicaragua had been the volcanoes. Did not the Nicaraguan coat of arms feature a smoking volcano? And did not another appear on the postage stamp then in current use?[4] Would a country feature on

4

its national emblems something which was not characteristic of its national life? When Nicaragua protested loudly that there was not a shred of evidence to indicate volcanic activity within a hundred miles of the proposed canal, the Panama lobby was able to point to the nearby island of Martinique, where only a few weeks before a volcano had erupted and, in two cataclysmic minutes, destroyed the whole town of St Pierre. Thirty thousand died! Did the world want a canal vulnerable to such natural disasters?

By such a margin, and for such reasons, did Nicaragua fail to become a major crossroads of the world.

* * * * *

But it is not only on the international scene that the promise of the San Juan has remained unfulfilled. Nicaragua herself has failed to treat the river with the respect it deserves. The colonising Spaniards came to Nicaragua up the isthmus from Panama and not from the Atlantic. They settled the fertile lands to the west around the country's great lakes, and were little interested in the seemingly impenetrable rain forest to the east. On its far side lay the Caribbean shore, where indigenous tribespeople continued to live untouched by this colonial 'invasion'. These people were finally befriended – doubtless from motives of both anti-Spanish sentiment and self-interest – by the British, who set up a 'protectorate'. Hence, Nicaragua has suffered, and still suffers, a serious lack of political and cultural cohesion between its eastern and western seaboards.

Pedro Chamorro, a well-known newspaper editor, who died in 1978, developed a love affair for this south-east corner of his native land. The forested length of the San Juan is of unspoiled beauty: 'A place of almost sacred solitude,' wrote José Coronel Urtecho. Pedro would take his family launch across the lake, saddened to see the lonely river draining prosaically to the ocean, forgotten and abandoned. He has been one of very few Nicaraguans who have ever recognised the potential importance of the area or sought to alert his fellow countrymen and women to the illogicality of its neglect.

He saw the San Juan river and the great lakes as the country's 'hydrographic axis', and bemoaned the fact that politicians were abandoning an area which should have been the feet on which the nation stood. He could not believe that the country had 'turned her back' so blatantly on the realities of her own geography. The river could have been a doorway to the world. It was a doorway that had been allowed to stay closed for far too long. He was not to know that twelve years after his death his widow, doña Violeta, would be elected President of a country even more beset by problems than in his own day.

This story is about an attempt to show one way in which the river San Juan might be reopened, the whole region revitalised and a step taken towards a more meaningful integration of a divided country. It is a story about vision, Christian commitment and courage. It is also a story about taking risks in the search for progress.

Chapter 2

Rekindling Dreams

'Come back as soon as you can,' said the elegant, silver-haired grandmother as she leant forward in a rocking chair; these finely carved cedarwood chairs are a feature of many Nicaraguan homes and offices. On the wall behind her hung a portrait of a man striding purposefully forward. But this was no family visit to a retirement home. We were in the private office of the Nicaraguan Head of State in Government House, Managua, our hostess was none other than Violeta Barrios de Chamorro, President of the Republic and the portrait was of her late husband, Pedro Joaquín Chamorro. It was 1994, and we had been invited to outline before the President our proposals to use the unique technology of the hovercraft to open up communications in the south-east corner of her country.

We sat in a circle around doña Violeta, aware of a sudden animation in her face as the Project Leader, Michael Cole, touched on his desire to help the poor and under-privileged of Nicaragua, and in particular the children. The President explained how much she shared our compassion for the needy; she clearly felt a mother's love for the nation's children, as well as for her own.

'My husband wrote a book about the part of the country you want to explore. I've got a copy of it somewhere at home; I'll find it and send it to you.' The President's informality was delightful, and as we left we carried in our mind's eye a picture of her sifting carefully through the family bookshelves on our behalf. But we rationalised that, facing the weight of presidential responsibilities in a country still struggling to find its feet after a decade of civil war, the offer, however kindly meant, would prove too trivial a matter to be remembered.

We were wrong! Just a few weeks later a package arrived at Mike Cole's home in Herefordshire: a faded, original pamphlet containing the series of articles written by don Pedro and first published in 1970 by the *La Prensa* newspaper of which he was then editor: *Los Pies Descalzos de Nicaragua* (the Naked Feet of Nicaragua). The articles described don Pedro's travels along the San Juan river, and the unspoiled rain forest through which it flows. He saw the area as one which should have been a strong base on which Nicaragua could stand and develop, in fact as feet which the Republic had sadly allowed to go unshod. He also dreamt that one day technology might provide an answer. 'I cannot tell,' he mused, 'whether the answer will come in the form of a miraculous pair of seven-league boots or a more prosaic pair of sandals.' But Pedro Joaquín Chamorro was totally convinced that an answer had to be found if Nicaragua were ever to accept successfully the realities of her geography.

But his life was cut short. In 1978 he was assassinated, an atrocity that fanned flames of political revolt which, within a year, coalesced into a forest fire of revolution. The much hated Somoza regime was brought down, but a decade of no less baneful civil war was just around the corner. Pedro was not there to see it, or to bewail this further delay to the development of the region he loved so deeply. Reading his work we thought we knew why his widow had welcomed us so warmly. She was encouraging us to revive her husband's dream, inviting us, if we could, to fulfil his prophecy. For Mike and the team the challenge was unmistakable.

Yet it was children in the Managua market-place that had first brought us to the President's attention. Mrs Thelma Pereira is another woman with a heart for needy children. She had been particularly moved by the plight of unschooled children in one of Managua's main popular markets, the *mercado oriental*. Here the market women could not afford to send their children to school because they needed them to help run the family stall.

More seriously, Thelma discovered that abandoned children represented a fifth of the local population, orphaned as a result of civil war, drug abuse or violent crime in the very market area. Keenly aware of how vulnerable street kids are, and motivated by her Christian faith, in 1986 Thelma had recruited volunteers to promote free primary and pre-primary classes for sixty children. They had begun in rented premises right on the edge of the market. Two half-day sessions allowed children to attend school for one and work with their parents outside for the other.

By 1990 the initiative was so successful that the school employed twelve teachers and provided primary education for 500 youngsters daily. They called it 'Noah's Ark', since it was rescuing children from a sea of hopelessness all around. When she needed to develop her project still further Mrs Pereira got in touch with Dr John Kessler, a Dutchman who had for many years served the Christian churches of Latin America, and who was then in neighbouring Costa Rica.

When approached by Thelma, Kessler thought of the community project programme for young people started by the British mission with which he had once worked in Peru. The Short Term Experience Projects (STEPs) of Latin Link had begun as a response by a team of British young people to a cry for help from victims of terrorist violence in Peru. In 1984 a small community in the central Andes was devastated when six elders of the local church were brutally shot by government soldiers looking for terrorists of *Sendero Luminoso* (Shining Path). As the military struggled to combat the growing reign of terrorism, innocent people were caught in the crossfire. The incident provoked a national church project to find safe sanctuary for such victims. When Mike Cole, then a serving officer in the Royal Air Force, learnt that they were being housed in a crowded church hall in Lima, he responded by raising an ad hoc team of sixteen Christian volunteers, including his own son, daughter, brother and nephew. They moved in in the summer of 1985, with energy and commitment, to install a water supply and build essential bridges to a refugee village in the remote high jungle. Their enthusiasm and dedication lifted the morale of a depressed community, and gave real meaning to a name which had earlier been no more than an expression of yearning. The village was called Paz y Esperanza or Peace and Hope.

Peruvian leaders and the British Ambassador were present when the bridges were completed and inaugurated in 1985, together with a certain Dr David Milnes, MC. David had lost an eye while serving in the RAMC at El Alamein in 1942, and won the Military Cross. After the war he became a medical missionary in the Andes of Peru. Now seventy years of age, he had watched the young STEP team provide a beacon of hope for a people he loved. He tapped Mike on the shoulder and whispered: 'We must give many more British youngsters an opportunity to serve like this!'

So the possibility of what later became the STEP programme was born. Mike resigned his RAF commission and joined Latin Link in order to develop the vision. Since 1985, 150 such projects have been completed among needy communities of Argentina, Bolivia, Brazil, Ecuador, Mexico and Peru. D-Day veteran Douglas Edmonds, RNVR, led the task in Bolivia. John Kessler, knowing Mike's priorities were for the 'poorest of the poor', put him in touch with Thelma, and challenged him to take STEP to Nicaragua, a republic bruised and aching after a decade of Sandinista/Contra conflict, and by then the poorest nation on the mainland of Latin America.

As a result, a team of eleven young people, mostly students during their long vacation, worked alongside half a dozen Nicaraguan volunteers to build a multi-purpose assembly hall at the Noah's Ark school during the summer of 1991. Mrs Pereira put the Steppers up in her own home and arranged for them to be escorted to the building site each day through the market-place, an area the locals judged at the time too dangerous for unaccompanied foreigners. Managua was still a volatile location, although the war had officially been over for a couple of years. The team was led by a sparkling twenty-two-year-old language student, Amanda Lee, who rapidly adapted her fluent Italian into the local Spanish.

They were invited to lead Sunday worship in Managua jail. 'You don't know what it's like to be holed up in a place like this,' remarked one of the prisoners. One of the Steppers, an ex-prisoner himself, now reformed and youth leader of his church in the UK, stood forward and spoke with great clarity of the changing power of Christ. In every sense this first STEP team in Nicaragua in 1991 was radical and life-changing.

The British Ambassador was astonished to find his expatriate community more than doubled overnight, and made a note to visit them to check how his new charges were coping with Managua. When he did he was so impressed by their commitment that he left indications that his imminent successor would be justified in adopting a positive attitude towards any funding requests. Mike happened to be making a supervisory visit to the team when he called in. As they chatted, the Ambassador realised that the STEP director was the same man who had led a hovercraft expedition to Nepal some years previously. He had read Mike's book[1] and ventured to suggest that he should make the river San Juan the next focus for his vision of using hovercraft to open up communication and bring medical help to isolated communities. In fact Mike had only just completed a major expedition to China in 1990,[2] and was in the thick of preparations for another to Papua New Guinea in 1993.[3] But he filed the suggestion at the back of his mind as he concentrated on the tasks immediately to hand.

By 1993 the new Ambassador in Managua, HE John Culver, alerted by the files of his predecessor, found generous grants for STEP building materials for 1993 and 1994, and encouraged Mike to follow up the suggestion about the river San Juan. He also drew his attention to the unusual culture of the eastern coast of Nicaragua, and to British historical connections there.

* * * * *

The Atlantic coast has been known as the Mosquito Shore, *Mosquitía* in Spanish. Although Colombus 'discovered' a cape on this coast during one of his later meanderings through

11

the Caribbean, the Spanish colonisers did not arrive from the Atlantic. They found the jungle to the east forbidding and made little or no attempt to colonise it.

The 'Mosquito Coast' may seem an altogether appropriate name for an area where malaria and dengue have always been – and still are – uncomfortably prevalent. But, strangely, the name has nothing to do with the mosquito, being apparently a linguistic perversion of the name of the major race indigenous to the area, the Miskitos.

From the first, these people felt a strong antipathy to the invading Spaniards, who came in as it were behind their back. They were a tall race, well built but nimble, and made excellent hunters with spears and harpoons. Buccaneers in the 17th century were quick to note their hatred of things Spanish, and often made contact from the sea, recruiting them as allies for their marauding expeditions. They found them bold and loyal.

Later visits of the British navy to the Mosquito Shore were met at first with some suspicion, but the Miskitos finally became extraordinarily attached to England and, over a considerable period, actually acknowledged the English Sovereign as their own. At least one historian judged them 'the best affected and most constant of all the friends that Britain ever had'.[4]

Before the 19th century two or three hundred British settlers had moved on to the coast with other natives of the Caribbean islands, introducing the English language together with other elements of British culture. This has complicated still further the integration of the Caribbean area into the rest of modern Nicaragua, which was already difficult enough, given its geographical isolation and the deep-seated Miskito resentment of the colonisers. They were in general so strongly opposed to Nicaraguan rule that some fled to Jamaica, and fought from there for their political independence. One document still lying in British diplomatic archives declares: 'Shall we swear allegiance to Nicaragua? We say no, emphatically no, a thousand times no! . . . Men, women, children, young and old cry aloud with the sound of thunder: No, no, no, ever no. A thousand times, no!' One gathers they were opposed to the idea!

But the die had been cast. For Britain to have taken up heavier political cudgels in the cause of the Miskito people, a vital factor was missing, namely, an adequate degree of British self-interest. What was Britain to get out of a desolate stretch of Central American coastline? On such factors, rather than on thoughts of altruism, have the bounds of Empire – and even of international justice – too often been drawn. A British legation as late as 1951 was still deploring the sadness of the Mosquito Coast, and that 'The incorporation (into Nicaragua) has not really taken place . . . the Atlantic coast is still either ignored by Managua, or treated as a tiresome encumbrance.' They concluded: 'The British tradition in this strange English-speaking territory still survives.'

Today, a generation later, that tradition is fading, yet full integration into Nicaraguan life still awaits. Not even today can one travel from Managua to Bluefields on the coast all the way by road, though scarcely 200 miles apart. It is this abysmal lack of communication across the isolating rain forest, more than any other one factor, which forms a persistent barrier to social progress on the Mosquito Coast. After nearly 500 years, mutual understanding has yet to be achieved between the people of the eastern lowlands and the bulk of the population settled in the highlands to the west. As one American historian has put it: 'For the Miskitos and Creoles of the east, the true foreigners and outsiders have been not from overseas but from the other side of the rain forest.'[5]

As a result, the people of the Atlantic coast showed little interest in the long struggle against the Somoza dictatorship, though finally it was uniting everywhere else the left, right and centre of Nicaraguan politics, rich and poor, town and country. Nor did they show much interest in the revolutionary government which followed, so when the Sandinistas meted out some brutal treatment to the Miskitos it did nothing whatever to lessen the long-standing animosities. The people of the coast complained that they had always been poor, but that now the 'Sandinistas had given them misery to contend with as well'.

*   *   *   *   *

In 1992 Freddy Zamorán, the enthusiastic Nicaraguan director of social projects for churches of the Central America Mission, had successfully arranged for STEP volunteers to build some classrooms at a Christian school and vocational centre on the volcanic island of Ometepe in the middle of Lake Nicaragua. So Mike approached him again to ask whether anything similar could be done on the Caribbean coast. The outcome was an introduction to Ed Jaentschke, a pastor of the Verbo congregation in Bluefields, a small port some hundred miles north of Greytown. The denomination was already running a centre outside Managua where young people were learning farming skills in a caring Christian environment, and an effort had been made to duplicate the idea in Bluefields. By 1994 Ed had made a promising start with the purchase of suitable land on the edge of the town. But it was proving difficult to find viable employment for the young men, who consequently tended to drift in and out of the project. And in 1988, when Bluefielders were already struggling to rebuild their lives after the war, much of the area was flattened by Hurricane Joan, leaving the population badly dispirited. It was just the kind of situation in which STEP could be a catalyst to dispel the inertia.

'You're welcome, brother,' beamed Pastor Ed, his huge smile flashing beneath the peak of a baseball cap as he greeted Mike on the tarmac of Bluefields' tiny airport. 'The young people is working hard on the farm, though it rain so much and there is plenty mud.' For Mike, too active a man to sit and study Spanish comprehensively, it was a delight to hear the Creole English – not that lack of Spanish had ever hindered his initiative or energy!

As Ed drove him in a battered pick-up along the rutted streets, splashing through pools of red mud, the contrast with the rest of Nicaragua which Mike had been led to expect was evident. Most people around were of Caribbean appearance, some strikingly Caribbean-Indian, descendants of the original indigenous coastal tribes, Miskitos, Ramas and Sumos.

As they arrived at the church farm on a hillside above the town a strange rumble presaged a storm. A grey curtain of water was moving towards them across the corrugated iron roofs below. In a matter of seconds the drumming became deafening as the torrents of rain reached the farm buildings. Mike expected the Steppers working down below him to run for cover, but no one moved. 'We'd waste so much time if we stopped every time it rains. Anyway, it's so hot our clothes dry out almost immediately,' grinned a volunteer, rain splashing from his hair and face, T-shirt plastered to chest, and legs smeared with mud and cement down to the wellies. 'We're learning to mix the mortar a bit on the dry side. If there's a sudden shower it doesn't run out from between the bricks!'

The Steppers were helping Ed's congregation to build a pig-barn with a view to starting a project which would give a regular income to the farm and its workers. Others could also learn pig husbandry, and begin their own schemes by borrowing a sow from the farm. Many locals had not bothered to rebuild their homes since the hurricane, afraid that the next storm would flatten them anyway. So the team and their Nicaraguan friends had decided that the pig unit should be a substantial structure of cement blocks as well as timber. If the barn withstood the rainy season it would show the wider community what was possible.

The friendship between the British team and the church in Bluefields went much deeper than a pig-pen. A number of the Steppers from traditional churches in the UK had their Christian outlook expanded not only by the liveliness of the Pentecostal worship – Creole-style rhythm and exuberance! – but also by the gentle but profound challenge of Pastor Ed's Bible teaching. Several team members asked to be baptised by Ed to mark their renewed Christian commitment. It was thrilling to see British young people accepting and responding to spiritual leadership from a Latin American pastor. This is a powerful demonstration of today's understanding of Christian mission as a two-way affair. Third World churches certainly deserve to get help from our material 'overflow', but

15

indisputably they have a spiritual 'overflow' from which we can benefit too. Is this not what the Apostle Paul meant when he wrote about wanting equality (2 Cor. 8:14)?

That summer Mike attended the official opening of a Christian primary school at Los Brasiles near Managua, where another STEP team had helped to build the first classroom block. Members of the local congregation had completed the work, the British Embassy chipping in with desks and blackboards. As the Ambassador's contact with the Steppers had grown, so had his confidence in the programme. He inaugurated the buildings in the presence of a large crowd which included the intriguingly named Señor Sandino, Vice-Minister of Education. STEP was obviously beginning to have a much wider impact on the nation than had ever been anticipated.

In early 1994 John Culver had invited Pedro Chamorro Junior to an informal supper in the Embassy. This was the ebullient son of the Nicaraguan President, named after the father who had written the 'naked feet' articles. Over the meal the idea of hovercraft on the river San Juan came up again. 'I must tell my mother about this!' said Pedro. A few days later this relaxed conversation had become a full-length article in *La Prensa*, where Pedro was among the editors. 'THE ENGLISH ARE COMING BACK TO THE RIVER SAN JUAN' ran the headline, recalling an ill-fated 1780 British naval expedition under a certain Captain Nelson. 'This time they will be coming in peace,' Pedro had written.

Thursday, 21 April 1994, was a remarkable day. Into the morning's activities were telescoped the achievements of the previous four years and the potential of the next four. At 9 o'clock the project's planning team joined the British Ambassador at the Noah's Ark school for the inauguration of a new kitchen and dining-room. The school had been trying to provide a basic daily lunch for its children, although it had had to be cooked in the open air. Impressed by a project which now touched a total of 700 children, and employed twenty-two full-time Christian staff, John Culver had helped provide some greatly improved facilities. It was difficult not to be moved

Doña Violeta Barrios de Chamorro, President of
the Republic of Nicaragua.

'Sympathy is no substitute for action'. David Livingstone

Captain David Milnes MC
RAMC, EL Alamein, 1942,
then Peru.

Squadron Leader Michael Cole
OBE, Project Leader.

Sub-lieutenant Douglas Edmonds RNVR, D-Day, Normandy, 1944. Later STEP Co-ordinator in Bolivia.

Squadron Leader Dick Bell. In 1968, the RAF's top aerobatic pilot.

Wing Commander Peter Dixon, RAF.

Nick Cole at the Coniston 14 – gruelling but rewarding.

The centenary celebration at the Houses of Parliament of the
handover of Mosquito Shore.

The Rusting Hulk – a monument to the abortive attempt to
cut a canal across the isthmus.

On the Mosquito Shore. 'Man, you can't go this way!'

Gareth repairs the skirt.

Essential maintenance at the hovergarage at Bluefields.

Opening the school at Bluefields.
The VIPs were late but nobody minded.

The vocational centre in Nueva Guinea.

Pioneers: Pastor Ed Jaentschke and young explorer David Coates.

'The water's dry, very dry.'

by the excitement of hundreds of children as they sang their welcome, expressed their gratitude, and scrambled and jostled at the end for photo-calls with their friends. They were being given hope, so different from the grey sadness of people struggling to make a living in the crowded, crime-racked squalor of the market the other side of the wall; 'Noah's Ark' was afloat and surviving the flood!

From there a five-minute drive transported the party to another world. Pedro had indeed spoken to his mother, and the result was a call to meet with Violeta Barrios de Chamorro, President of the Republic, in her quiet air-conditioned offices at Government House. We assumed it had been planned as a brief opportunity for her to express polite interest in the proposals. But, in the event, she listened and questioned, together with several of her ministers, for a full hour about STEP, hovercraft and the river San Juan. Thinking of the contribution made to the educational scene, she turned to Mike personally: 'As a woman and a Christian, and in the name of the Nicaraguan people,' she said, 'I thank you and your volunteers for your generous initiatives.' Thinking of the proposed cross-isthmus journey she added: 'I shall hope to welcome the hovercraft personally, and I promise all the help that I or my ministers can give.' She graciously agreed to be named Patron of the project, and Mike promised to return as soon as he could.

Chapter 3

Hover Fever

'I'm just an ordinary pastor,' began Freddy Zamorán, as he stood apprehensively before a packed meeting at the Royal Geographical Society in Kensington Gore, London, in December 1993. Over seven hundred supporters and friends had gathered for the launch of *Beyond the Lagoon*, the book about the 'hoverdoctor' project to Papua New Guinea undertaken earlier that year. Freddy had been whisked straight from Heathrow. The formality of the oak-panelled auditorium, with its plush seats and names of famous British explorers carved in a roll of honour along the balcony, must have presented a sharp contrast to the simple church gatherings in the hinterland of Nicaragua to which Freddy was more accustomed. He welcomed the hovercraft project which Mike had just announced, and spoke with great feeling of the needs of his country. As he thanked Britain for the help already given by the STEP teams the openness and enthusiasm of the audience rose in response.

Mike was unlikely to be intimidated by the location. Pointing to the names of Stanley and Livingstone on the balcony, he gave a characteristic challenge: 'These were great Christians who founded the British traditions of adventure and exploration. Their calling to do something about the physical and spiritual poverty of man became inescapable. It was Livingstone who said: "Sympathy is no substitute for action." Since then, Christians in Britain have, by and large, watched secular professionals take up that adventurous spirit in the name of science, technology and commerce. We aim to re-grasp the initiative and reclaim this Christian heritage in a small way by setting up in Nicaragua an "adventure with a purpose".'

'All very impressive,' thought his son Nick, as people crowded around afterwards, keen to get their hands on one of the glossy Nicaragua brochures just off the press, courtesy of BP. 'But at the moment this is all the project consists of!' However, adopting a stance to match the positive tone of the leaflet, he enthusiastically took names of people – many ex-Steppers – who wanted to register their interest. Here was a project combining the potential of committed youth with the technological possibilities of hovercraft, drawing on Mike's successful expeditions elsewhere in the world.

* * * * *

Back in 1982 Mike was about to take his fourteen-year-old son Nick on a skiing trip when an urgent need to visit Peru in preparation for a hovercraft expedition to the Amazon[1] obliged him to cancel. But he had always wanted his children to share his vision for overseas mission, so Nick's itinerary was switched from Aviemore to Lima. Some years later both Nick and his sister Carolyn were encouraged to join the team heading for the Peace and Hope camp in Peru. It was there that Nick first experienced the risks as well as the joys of radical Christian service.

'As we crawled out of our tents in the jungle after an overnight stop *en route* to the refugee camp, we were confronted by an army patrol entering the clearing, each soldier with a sub-machine-gun slung over his shoulder. They were *sinchis*, specially trained commandos of Peru's anti-terrorist force, and had been sent to check us out. We might have been planning to set up a jungle training camp for guerrillas! They insisted on escorting us to the refugee settlement and we set off uneasily. When we wobbled so unsteadily on a couple of tree-trunks to cross a jungle stream the *sinchis* must have seen that we were no more than we claimed to be! But the tension only eased when one of them stumbled into an ants' nest and danced around trying to rid himself of the menace. Once satisfied by their enquiries at Peace and Hope they marched back into the jungle leaving the crazy "gringos"[2] to get on with it.'

Later, when a student at Cambridge, in 1989 Nick led a STEP team to the *villas de miseria* (Townships of Need) in Buenos Aires, with Britain and Argentina still technically at war over the Falklands/Malvinas. The Argentinian press chose to describe the British team who were working alongside local Christians to build a street-kids' centre as 'Ambassadors for Peace'.

* * * * *

By 1993 Nick had moved from his position as a management trainee to work full-time with his father, and that year joined him on his visit to Nicaragua. They flew, with the British Ambassador, low-level along the length of the river San Juan. The rapids and sandbanks – the San Juan's peculiar problem – were clearly visible. Equally clearly, it was most unlikely that they would present any problem to a hovercraft. In which case, Pedro Chamorro was right – a forgotten backwater that had once caught the imagination of sailors and engineers the world over could, and should, be opened up again to bring the lush Caribbean within reach of the rest of the Republic and to make it that much easier for Nicaragua to become the single integrated nation that atlases and textbooks the world over have long assumed it to be.

Mike began to get the project into a truer perspective. Humanitarian need had first brought him to Nicaragua, the starving and the homeless, the widows and the orphans, and even now he was determined that they would not be forgotten. But he came to appreciate that day the long-term benefits that could accrue if technology could open up the river. He was often tempted to think of people as much more important than hovercraft *per se*, but from that moment on he remembered that, properly understood, this was going to be a communication project, and the long-term objectives had to be kept in mind.

Nick, a spectator of hovercraft projects throughout his earlier years, was thrilled at the prospect of active participation at last. 'Sign me up, Dad!' was his verdict.

'More than half the work of any expedition is in the planning' was a caveat Nick had often heard, and was often to pass on to potential team members in the next few months. 'It's no use just showing up at the airport with your rucksack; we need people whose total commitment will start promoting the project right now,' he explained to the first applicant interviewed. It was evident that there would be no shortage of volunteers, nor would they be much dissuaded by the obligation each one faced of personally raising a sum towards project costs. But the task of raising the capital sum required by the whole project threatened to be an uphill struggle.

BP had given substantial fuel sponsorship to the Papua New Guinea project, but there Mike was dealing with the business growth area of the Asia–Pacific rim. This had been even more so on the China expedition, when the multinationals had almost elbowed each other out of the way in their enthusiasm to support him. But Nicaragua? BP had no business operation there. Who did? Nicaragua seemed almost non-existent as far as British exporters were concerned. It was viewed, if viewed at all, as an exclusively North American sphere, and the historic British links with the Mosquito Shore were just that, and no more.

Progress on team recruitment remained positive. Given the exceptional degree of interest developing within Nicaragua itself, Mike realised that the project needed a staff worker based in Managua throughout the preparation period. Sarah Lister had pioneered a STEP project to the slums of Mexico City in 1991, and seemed just the person. When working in the PR department of a multinational shipping firm she had skilfully persuaded her boss that leading a team of volunteers overseas would provide ideal training in people management. The year before she had gone to Bolivia when a seed of interest in Latin America's poor had been planted; in Mexico City that summer it took root and flourished. She returned to the UK and, resigning a promising career, swapped the arranging of

21

maritime photo-shoots on the Mersey for unassuming social work in the poverty of Mexico City. This was just the kind of radical, hands-on Christian commitment that Mike Cole was looking for, so he challenged Sarah to think of moving south to help the equally needy of Nicaragua by running the community projects, and undertaking there the anchor administrative role for the hovercraft project. By early 1994 she was helping Nick in the London STEP office and had set about raising personal financial support for Managua, while Mike himself had begun the gigantic task of fundraising for the purchase of the hovercraft.

All four previous expeditions had used six-seater River Rovers, designed and built by a group of Christian engineers who run a charitable organisation called Hoveraid. The early models were petrol-powered but, with diesel more readily available in the developing world, a new version had been pioneered in Papua New Guinea. The engineers had worked extremely hard to get the heavier diesel engine to deliver sufficient power to compensate for its extra weight without its being subject to overheating in the tropics. So Mike welcomed Hoveraid's intention of installing a potentially more powerful Land Rover engine in their latest design. Once the power unit from the internationally successful Defender-Discovery vehicles had been built into River Rover 501, his 'sponsorship antennae' were undoubtedly twitching at the thought of approaching a British company with strong Third World links.

On 24 January 1994 he sent an initial £100 deposit to Hoveraid, and formally ordered a River Rover for Nicaragua. This sum was a gift from the parish church of St Mawgan, Cornwall, where Stan Baldock, a distinguished retired RAF wing commander, is a member. Stan is also a talented artist and had produced great oils of the hovercraft in action both in Nepal and in China. He had been on the China project and it was now his infectious enthusiasm which resulted in the donation from his fellow parishioners. Though Hoveraid reduced the price as much as they could in view of the charitable nature of the operation, the deposit was a minute amount in relation to the thousands required. But the gift typified the hundreds of individuals who had supported the projects over nearly twenty years. And on the smaller gifts of such individual Christians the Nicaragua project might yet have to depend, rather than on large commercial sponsorships.

The aerial recce had revealed that the river was wide enough for larger craft, and Mike knew in his heart that an effective demonstration of the potential of hovercraft would not be possible while restricted to the limited payload of the River Rover. 'We need a Griffon,' he mused. He was thinking of June 1990 when he had stood on the roof of the world at the source of the Yangtze in Tibet. It was a Griffon 2000 TDX which had taken them there. 'They're the best in the world. If it had broken down out there we should probably still be walking out!' Mike was happy to joke about it now, but at the time the team had literally trusted their lives to the Griffon in some of the world's most hostile conditions. 'Nicaragua's rivers and lakes will be less demanding, and anyway it was a prototype we had in China. Griffon will have added some refinements since. It would be a powerful combination if the Griffon could show the payload potential on the main rivers while the River Rover was used to scout ahead and explore the narrower tributaries. The only problem . . . is money!'

A quick phone call to Graham Gifford, the affable sales manager of Griffon Hovercraft, and a good friend of the hoverdoctor projects, confirmed the likely price – a quarter of a million pounds! He promised that if we were seriously interested he would do his best to reduce it. Mike reflected; it had been done before in China. Could he manage to raise such money again?

But China had been an extremely close-run thing. Some people, Christians among them, had doubted Mike's wisdom in taking such risks on that occasion and, as had already been seen, the level of European interest in Nicaragua was much less. Furthermore, the China experience had been tough on Mike and had stretched even his considerable tenacity to the limits. The comfort zones of a man approaching his sixties might have suggested his leaving another such project to younger people. Weeks passed.

23

His feet might be getting older but his step of faith was no less firm. On 26 February 1994, compelled, as he believed, by the Spirit of God within him, by what he had seen personally of the suffering in Nicaragua, and by the affirmation of more and more Christian people who heard him speak across Britain, he ordered a Griffon 2000 TDX, and sent a £100 deposit to the company. This time the amount really was insignificant. Mike added a note: 'An earnest of the promise! I don't know as yet where the balance will be coming from.'

In March 1994, in the no man's land between winter and spring, an innocuous-looking fax arrived from the Foreign and Commonwealth Office. It was a telex from Ambassador Culver reporting that he had just had a most positive meeting with Nicaragua's Foreign Minister about the proposed expedition:

'. . . THE NICARAGUAN GOVERNMENT IS ENTHUSI-ASTIC. HIS MINISTRY WOULD PROVIDE WHATEVER ASSISTANCE IT COULD . . . PRESIDENT CHAMORRO WOULD WANT TO RECEIVE THE EXPEDITION LEADER AND HIS TEAM DURING THE RECCE VISIT.'

On that grey, dull morning it took Nick and Sarah several minutes to absorb the exciting news of this very real interest at the highest level of Nicaraguan government. They almost missed the brief line at the bottom of the telex:

'SHELL (NICARAGUA) HAVE AGREED TO SPONSOR ALL FUEL FOR THE EXPEDITION.'

This was major progress. That unexpected fax turned out to be the first sneeze of what, as it grew and grew, Mike came to refer to as 'hover fever in Nicaragua'.

On Easter Monday the team, now beginning to take shape, met for the first time at Gorsley Baptist Church, Ross-on-Wye, Mike Cole's local church. He judged it an early indication of commitment to see how many would be prepared to give up their bank holiday for a planning day. Almost thirty attended; a mixture of veterans from previous projects, ex-Steppers and other young volunteers interviewed in the previous few weeks.

A new feature was the presence of 'second generation' team members. In addition to Mike and Nick Cole, there were Peter and Matthew Dixon. In 1978, as a flight lieutenant, Peter had been one of the hover pilots on the Nepal project. On that occasion Mike had broken his rule of not allowing team members with children under two to join overseas teams, and agreed that Peter could leave baby Matthew at home with his wife. Sixteen years later that 'baby' was aiming to do something purposeful during his gap year before university. So he and his father, now wing commander in charge of the London University Air Squadron, planned to share together in the Nicaragua adventure.

Scanning the church hall, Mike started to think that the youthful energies of dynamic young people channelled by the skill and experience of a few 'grey-heads' might prove a powerful combination. Sitting in the front row were Dennis and Brenda Smith, who had spent their earlier lives in Peru with the Evangelical Union of South America (EUSA). After years with Dennis as head teacher of the *Colegio Internacional*, a leading school in Arequipa, the second city of Peru, they had come back to Britain where Dennis became the Mission's UK director until his retirement in 1991. He had been deeply involved in the founding of Latin Link and in recruiting Mike to set up and run the much needed STEP programme. Keen to support any new initiative for Christian mission in Latin America, Dennis and Brenda enquired tentatively: 'Could you use a couple of high-mileage pensioners? Well maintained – excellent runners over rough roads.' 'I need a Spanish interpreter,' said Mike, 'especially for our meeting with the President, so why not come on the recce and see? We're leaving for Nicaragua next week!'

Mike addressed the team. 'Team selection will be governed more by the practical commitment you show from now on than by your CVs. In a sense team members will select themselves. When can you begin? Right now.' Pointing to a five-foot-high stack of polythene-wrapped packs he challenged prospective volunteers to take away twenty copies of *Beyond the Lagoon* and fifty coasters which had been left over from Papua New Guinea fundraising. 'Be creative with these. When you talk to your friends or church members about the project get them to buy a coaster, and suggest that every day, when they lift their morning coffee off the hovercraft logo, they'll be reminded to pray for you and Nicaragua. The personal fundraising target for everyone participating is £2,500. That will cover all your personal costs on the expedition and will make a contribution as well both towards the capital needed and the project's admin costs.'

*   *   *   *   *

Those who went on the 1994 recce began to discover each other's strengths and weaknesses while in Nicaragua. The route from London involved changing planes in Houston. In the taxi from airport to local shopping mall Dennis Smith winced as Dick Bell launched into a characteristic conversation with the plump woman cab-driver. A jade statuette of the Bhudda dangled from the rear-view mirror – almost certainly no more than a decoration or a lucky charm for its owner – and Dick blurted out in a friendly sort of way: 'You know, you'd do yourself a real favour if you chucked that thing out of the window!' The driver tensed, then pretended not to hear. Dick shrugged his shoulders and settled back into the upholstery while Dennis shifted uneasily. Dick's approach had grated against years of living within, and learning to respect, other people's values, however bizarre they appeared to him.

Christ taught his followers to be 'fishers of men' (Matt. 4:19) but there are of course different ways of fishing. Some fish as if by dropping bricks in the river. But on the way back another of Dick's 'bricks' touched the soft spot of a burly chain-smoking driver, who warmly opened up about how hard his life had been since returning from Vietnam, and how for years his family had been unable to understand the struggle to readjust Stateside. Having disturbed him with his brick, Dick was quite gentle as he encouraged the bruised veteran to consider Christ's

offer of a life renewed and to seek out the support of Christian
people at a local church. 'There you go,' Dennis admitted, 'the
style may not be mine nor take into account the transcultural
niceties, but the Lord uses all sorts of willing witnesses, and
Dick's a special sort. There's no arguing about that!'

One of the main objectives of the planning visit was to travel
the 120-mile length of the Rio San Juan by conventional means.
The British Ambassador put the Embassy's four-wheel-drive at
our disposal for the five-hour journey round Lake Nicaragua,
from Managua to San Carlos at the head of the river – and,
incidentally, the end of the road! He also booked two outboard
canoes or *pangas* from the Ministry of Water Resources to take
the group downriver. Nick clambered aboard one, glancing
apprehensively at the spluttering outboard motor. He will
always remember the trip.

The Nicaraguan boatman, as weather-beaten as his
engine, gave a toothless grin. We couldn't entirely
share his confidence as we thought of the rapids and
sandbars ahead. It was the end of the dry season, so the
water level would be low, sandbanks on the silted-up
lower reaches at their most exposed and the five major
sets of rapids at their fiercest. As we churned round the
first bend the port of San Carlos seemed to slide listlessly
below the waters and, as if on cue, the rain began. Two
hours' hard driving against a stiff breeze brought us
to El Castillo. This is the ruined fort beside the river,
first built to deter pirates in the 17th century. As we
climbed the knoll behind the little settlement and stood
on the ramparts overlooking the river's most menacing
rapids we were well able to appreciate the strategic siting;
the fort commands a panoramic view of the river as it
disappears through the surrounding jungle towards the
Atlantic. After a night spent in the relative comfort of a
small lodge erected to attract tourists, we boarded again.
The experienced *pangueros* pointed the launches towards
the opposite bank to run the rapids through the calmest
channel. With the propellers lifted clear we were bounced

27

down largely at the mercy of the foaming current. After several hundred metres the water calmed but for some reason there was no acceleration. The boatman explained: '*El agua está seca, muy seca* (the water's dry, very dry).' Amused by the Spanish idiom we were soon to see just how 'dry' the water of the San Juan can be.

Downstream from El Castillo the San Juan forms the frontier with Costa Rica, and contrast between the banks is marked. On the Nicaraguan side, unbroken primary forest pulsates to the water's edge; in Costa Rica the jungle has mainly been cleared for cattle ranches and plantations, and the Nicaraguans are not well pleased at the river pollution caused by these *Tico* developments. (There is little love lost between the neighbouring peoples. Nicaraguan's refer to Costa Ricans somewhat disdainfully as *Ticos* and Costa Ricans get their own back by dubbing Nicaraguans *Nicos*.)

Eventually the bright green tangle of the jungle pressed in on both sides. A splash ahead brought them the magnificent sight of a jaguar swimming the river, pausing only to stare at the intruders. Here was a reminder of the priceless ecosystem of one of the world's last unspoilt rain forests. The Ministries of Environment and Tourism had already asked about the potential of hovercraft in promoting ecotourism in the area. A communication link by hovercraft would certainly delay, perhaps even prevent, a muddy road being gouged through the jungle.

Downriver the party was drenched by bursts of tropical rain then baked by equally tropical sun. Progress was slowed by the meanders of the river as, growing shallower by the mile, it searched out haphazardly its inevitable course to the sea. Six hours after leaving El Castillo, they had survived – despite ominous gratings of propellers on rocks – four sets of rapids, and reached the head of the delta, which according to the map is only some twenty miles from the Caribbean. But now sandbanks loomed increasingly across the bends and the water level dropped regularly to a few inches.

The engine coughed and choked dead, a churning froth of

black mud surrounding the stern. The hull scraped and the *panga* lurched to a stop, gently tilting in the current. The *panguero*, together with Nick and a couple of others, leapt over the side to heave the boat off the sandbar. There was no other way. The river hardly reached above their ankles, so the freshwater sharks they had heard much about were hardly a threat. Back on board they watched tensely as the engine was coaxed back to life, a procedure to be repeated several times over the next four hours.

After one such incident Nick was rehearsing the party's contingency plans of walking out with machetes through Costa Rica. For when the outboard was lifted, the propeller was missing! The pin had sheared. Their rising panic subsided when the *panguero* grovelled underwater and found it, then rose sharply again when it became clear that he was not carrying a spare pin! But, as is invariably the case in Latin America, ingenuity replaced foresight, and a bent and rusty nail found lying on the bottom of the *panga* provided the answer!

At last they broke through to the ocean. The jungle fell back, a high sandbank rose to replace it, and the surf could be heard crashing on the other side. Plumes of white spray were being hurled into the air at the bar where the river current meets the ocean tide. But they turned north into the peace of a lagoon which forms a natural harbour behind the coastal strip.

Very soon (remembers Nick), a small jetty came into view and as we tied up alongside a double row of simple wooden homes in the jungle clearing, an Afro-Caribbean with a dark bushy beard stepped hesitantly forward and greeted us in English: 'I heard you was comin'; my name is Aldrick Beckford. Welcome to Greytown.' At one of the remotest spots in Latin America he had spoken to us in English, and had used the old English name for the place. He had heard about our intended visit when visiting El Castillo, but when we asked about his English he replied proudly: 'Everyone in Greytown speak English. My grandfather come from Jamaica eighty years ago. My father and I both grow up here. It was all abandoned

during the war but now people has started comin'
back.' Everything about Aldrick confirmed the cultural
differences we had been led to expect on the coast.

After a meal of rice, beans and plantains, Aldrick introduced
them to the village mayor, Mariano. There are now some sixty
families in the community, including forty-seven children at
the primary school. Nick remembers asking about medical
services. 'A doctor visits us once a year – sometimes,' he
replied, and mentioned that two local children had died from
snakebite within the past month. In emergencies a *panga* has to
take the needy down the coast into Costa Rica and then by plane
to hospital in San José, assuming the patient can afford the fuel
for the boat – and the cost of chartering a light plane!
    They discussed the possibility of the journey time from San
Carlos being cut from the twelve hours it had just taken them
to three and a half by hovercraft. Faint glimmers of hope lit up
the faces of the community leaders. Here was the possibility of
Greytown benefiting from the medical services – such as they
are – which operate out of San Carlos; the possibility too of
officials from Managua visiting to learn first-hand about the
community's needs. Mike knew that these glimmers of hope
would soon fade if the strange machine they were struggling
to describe to the locals was not actually soon to be taken there.
How many times before had promises remained unfulfilled!
Seeing the abandoned state of the region had raised for him
both the height of the mountain to be climbed and his
determination to climb it.
    With the township now no more than a rural refugee
settlement, there was clearly no 'hotel' available, so the party
of six stayed in Aldric's modest home and used two of his
hammocks, with the one carry-mat they had with them. There
were plenty of mosquito nets. As the rain hammered down on
the tin roof they struggled to get comfortable on the warped
planks their host had thoughtfully laid out on the dirt floor.
During the fairly sleepless hours that followed Mike tried to
keep spirits high. 'I did promise you "full board",' he was
heard to quip, at two in the morning.

One startling surprise awaited them next morning. Before leaving they tried to pay a woman who had cooked their meal, only to find that she rejected their Nicaraguan currency, *córdobas*, and asked for Costa Rican *colones* instead. It was remarkable that these Nicaraguans should be forced into the position of being unable to use the coins of their realm. The fact underlined uniquely Nicaragua's urgent need of resolving the communication problem on the San Juan. Mike thought that the telling of the incident in Managua ought to cause the politicians some embarrassment and heighten their perception of the importance of the project. It had certainly heightened his.

They promised to return in a year's time, but not before having prayed together that in some way they could be used by God in this sad spot. Dick Bell, accustomed to pray in a language as intimate as it is colloquial – as a man talks to his friend in fact – was heard to plead: 'Father, you see us here in this place; grey by name and grey by nature. Won't you send to Greytown a little of the sunshine of your love? It needs it, Lord!' He was right. On that day at least, the sea was grey, so were the sandbars, so were the people in their rude homes, grey with the sadness and uncertainty of what the future might hold for them. Could the British Hovercraft Project bring a revival of fortune to a place so sadly cut off from its more colourful past?

As we sped across the lagoon (remembers Nick), we braced ourselves for heaving *pangas* off sandbanks again. This time we had to climb laboriously up the rapids we had almost bounced down the previous day. The Machucas, named after the first Spanish explorer to travel down the river in 1539, are the longest rapids and the nearest to the coast, so we faced the toughest test first. For more than a quarter of a mile, the current rakes a giant harrow of spitting white water across the rock and gravel bed. *Pangueros* face a dilemma. You endanger your engine if it strikes a boulder at high revs, but you stand little chance of reaching the top without

31

full power. Ours compromised with a medium throttle. We edged slowly forward to the foot of the rapid and stopped as the bows bit into the teeth of the current. The driver jabbed the throttle as though whipping forward a frightened horse, while I deliberately looked away from the rocks to concentrate on a tree on the bank a few yards ahead. It seemed to take an eternity to draw level and inch past. At times the outboard shuddered, and our boatman had to give the engine respite and allow the current to push us briefly backward before renewing the assault. Eventually, and quite suddenly, we were released from the rapid's grip. But the ordeal was to be suffered four times that day.

In the late afternoon, after a gruelling ten hours on the river, they arrived gratefully at El Castillo, then on to San Carlos, where they had a chance to assess weather conditions on the huge lake itself. When they crossed for a brief visit to the nearby islands of Solentiname, the prevailing easterly stiffened considerably, and the launches needed full throttle to get back through buffeting waves. The lake's weather (as is common with inland seas) was obviously volatile, and Mike noted that he would be wise to follow the sheltered eastern coastline with the hovercraft and to start each day's operations at first light.

The Missionary Aviation Fellowship (MAF) flew the team back to Managua. As Mike Cole sat with his six-foot frame squashed into a passenger seat on the Cessna, he got out the map and traced his finger up the eastern shore of Lake Nicaragua. Suddenly he paused and began tapping a point at the lake's north-east corner. He had noticed a river estuary, and following the blue line northwards saw that it almost reached the shore of Nicaragua's second largest lake, which is named after the capital city on its southern shore. 'What does that say, Nick?' Mike shouted over the engine noise, as he pointed to the tiny writing on the map. 'Tipitapa,' Nick replied. 'Ask the pilot to tell us when we get there,' continued Mike as the significance of what he had spotted began to sink in. 'If this river used to connect the two lakes, then it's possible we could test the amphibious properties of hovercraft to traverse the dried-up bed and reopen the link! It would also be a marvellous final leg of the hover journey to get all the way to Managua from the Atlantic via the San Juan. That would be highly significant, given the lack of integration between the country's two divided halves.' At the pilot's signal Mike caught sight of the mouth of the Tipitapa river. To the north the water turned a brilliant green at a point much earlier than the map indicated. 'I wonder,' he mused.

* * * * *

'We call it *lechuga* – how do you say? Lettuce,' explained Carlos Coronel, leaning against the gate post of his Tipitapa cattle ranch and pointing to the mat of water-weed which blocked the river below his farm. On closer inspection it resembled lettuce only in colour and shape; the leaves were thick and fibrous and beneath lay a substantial clod of roots. 'In the rainy season,' Carlos went on, 'the prevailing wind can blow up to five kilometres of the stuff up the river. The river's underneath but it's impossible to drive a *panga* through it.' Mike smiled as he recalled the River Rover tackling water-weed on lagoons in Papua New Guinea. 'Don't worry, Carlos. Provided we keep up our momentum the *lechuga* will be no problem for the hovercraft. We'll go over the top!'

The carpet of *lechuga* blended first into reeds then into scrubby pastureland. Several miles upstream from the ranch, the river had disappeared completely and cattle were grazing in the shade of substantial trees growing out of the bed of the old river. Even Dick Bell's customary optimism was a little dented. 'I might just struggle to steer the Griffon round that lot,' he ventured. 'But there are some fairly hefty boulders strewn around. How about using the road we've just driven down from Tipitapa town? I know it's crazy but we could haul the hovercraft out here and use its amphibious capability to drive overland to Lake Managua.'

'It's a thought, but we'll have to think about it very carefully,' replied Mike steadily. Hovercraft are fine across fields but there could be a problem on cambered roads. The prospect of a quarter of a million pounds' worth – and five tonnes – of machine careering about among people, cattle herds and vehicles along six miles of Nicaraguan track and a section of the Pan-American highway was not immediately appealing. He recognised sadly that the idea of linking the two great lakes might prove 'a bridge too far'.

*   *   *   *   *

Meanwhile the Ambassador's efforts to muster as much interest and support as he could culminated in an official reception at the residence in the evening of the day that President Chamorro had given the team an audience. Her son Pedro, together with other prominent Managuans, including more Cabinet ministers, listened attentively and then plied Mike with questions as he gave a slide presentation of what was being proposed. A few days earlier, over a private luncheon, the local general managers of Shell and Kodak had confirmed their support with fuel and film from their respective companies.

A TV crew and journalists had pounced on Mike that morning outside the President's office, so the visit was comprehensively featured on television and in national newspapers, including another front page in *La Prensa*. The symptoms were clear. Whether over rice and beans in Greytown, cocktails at the Embassy, or lobster thermidor at Managua's top French restaurant, 'hover fever' was taking hold in Nicaragua.

Chapter 4

Cold Sweat

Back in the UK Mike received a letter from David Heathcote-Amory, then Foreign Officer Minister for Latin American Affairs: 'We have given President Chamorro and her government our support during this period and your project will demonstrate graphically Britain's continued interest in Nicaragua's development . . . I feel sure there will be many UK companies . . . who will be prepared to support you.' He sent a copy of it to a helpful employee at Shell who was trying to get the director responsible for his company's charitable grants to look at an application.

Mike also enjoyed an early opportunity to meet with officials at the Foreign Office to explain our vision. At the time, one of the government's avowed priorities for an aid package was to favour the emerging democracies and the poorest of the world's nations. That augured well, for Nicaragua surely matched both descriptions. Furthermore, although not a major objective of the project, introducing Central America to hovercraft might well give British industry a chance to boost a British invention. 'My team are working hard to raise funds for the River Rover,' Mike informed the Latin American desk, 'we just need your help to acquire the Griffon.'

Selling his vision has undoubtedly been one of Mike's outstanding skills. The faces of the civil servants were as inscrutable as one would have expected, but they were impressed enough to encourage an application to the Overseas Development Administration (ODA) for joint funding, where the voluntary agency's contribution is matched pound for pound with government money.

On Thursday, 21 July, Mike boarded a train for London to attend what he saw as a crucial event, a farewell luncheon at the Foreign Office for the retiring Nicaraguan Ambassador to the UK. He had been careful to slip some copies of Heathcote-Amory's letter into his briefcase. When he picked up the day's newspaper it was to find that John Major's long-awaited reshuffle was headline news. No Cabinet heads had rolled but halfway down a longish list of middle-ranking changes Mike's eye caught the name of David Heathcote-Amory 'who crosses to the Treasury as Paymaster General'. His spirit sank. Overnight a key Foreign Office contact had been taken from him, and much of the significance of the appointment he was heading for had been lost. He would have to start all over again, and – he admitted to himself – the prospect of another opportunity to meet the minister responsible face to face had to be remote.

The rattle of automatic rifle shots shattered the stillness of the summer afternoon! '*No corre,* don't run . . . and now the *guardia* are attacking this particular district. They're pouring in heavy machine-gun fire . . . there's the crack of a sniper as well.' More bursts of gunfire, exploding shells and the drone of planes. 'This is what it's like for these civilians – for the poor in their hovels here in the slums – when the *guardia* mounts an attack on the Sandinistas behind the barricades . . . This is Harold Briley, BBC, Managua.'

Harold stopped his tape recorder and explained to startled team members: 'That's a broadcast I recorded in 1979 at the height of the Nicaraguan revolution. I thought it would be good to give you some authentic background to the country you'll be visiting next year.' With the civil war over as recently as 1990, Nicaragua had not yet reached stability; the deep wounds could all too easily be reopened. So Mike hoped Harold's dramatic intervention might balance any unduly heady attitude among the volunteers. Nicaragua was not going to be a picnic. After reporting the Falklands/Malvinas conflict for the BBC, Harold had tracked down Mike Cole and his hovercraft team on the headwaters of the Amazon, among the primitive tribes of Peru. He reported what he saw as 'this second British Task Force with a radically different mission of peace and humanitarian endeavour', and from that point on became a good friend and supporter. Now retired, he volunteered to join the Nicaraguan team. In a long career of reporting hard news from the world's trouble spots – including Bangladesh, Iran, Nicaragua – describing the victims had always had to come first. Now he wanted to get involved in the action on the other side of the microphone. Mike grasped the offer; Harold's experience and his wealth of personal contacts would prove invaluable when dealing with high-profile situations.

STEP Nicaragua 1994 sent one team to Nueva Guinea, a frontier town on the edge of the jungle 180 miles from Managua, where Freddy Zamorán worked. Founded in 1965, the town saw heavy fighting during the war and Freddy himself lost his mother-in-law, shot while waiting for a bus. The war deprived families of breadwinners and, not seldom, churches of their leaders. So the pastor's vision was to provide a residential training centre for the area, where would-be Christian leaders could take vocational courses alongside their traditional studies in order to support themselves with a trade. The STEP team built dormitories.

A second team went to the volcanic island of Ometepe in Lake Nicaragua. When Freddy and Mike had visited the team working there the year before, people from a very isolated community the other side of the volcano trekked round to see what was going on. It was a group from a church in Mérida with their pastor Juan Morales. 'Couldn't we do something to help them next year?' asked Mike quietly. Freddy was not sure. 'Juan does need a village schoolroom, but it's too far. Living conditions would be even more basic for the team, and the water supply's worse than here. Can we consider going so remote?' Mike insisted on visiting the place anyway, which was typical of his tenacity – some might say stubbornness! Whether there was more to it than that, and God was leading him in a special way, Freddy was not to know. They hired the only available truck and bounced and slid the few muddy miles to the village 'round the back of the volcano'. Pastor Juan was so delighted to see them that he shinned to the top of a coconut palm, knocked down half a dozen shells, then, having topped them with a machete, passed them over with the Nicaraguan equivalent of: 'Have a coffee!'

Mike has always sought to aim for those that Latin society calls the *marginados* – which scarcely needs translating. Help given to places like Mérida has no strategic impact on the wider community, but if Christ were on Ometepe today he would go behind the volcano; he always looked for those his society thought of as 'outcasts'. There are hundreds of 'Juan Morales' around the world, leaders of the remotest communities who have neither the schooling nor the contacts to find the help they need. Aid organisations seldom get to hear of them, for they are never able to get, much less fill in and return, the bulky application papers. You only find 'Juan Morales' by trekking out to sit with him under his coconut tree and drink his 'coffee'.

Mike had already made up his mind. But back home in Britain he recognised the problem of how to provide transport for a team in such a remote location. One afternoon when walking the dog along a ridge near Ross-on-Wye a youngster shot past him on a mountain bike. 'What about that?' he thought. 'That could be the answer for the rutted tracks of Ometepe.' The next evening, when guest speaker at the Rotary Club in nearby Newent, he shared the idea of a STEP team on mountain bikes. The novelty sparked an immediate response and the Rotarians donated four. Out in Managua Sarah approached the Raleigh agent and got two more; and a would-be Stepper in Peterborough boldly approached her local cycle store and got another! So the group was well equipped to pedal round the island, and when they had finished with the bikes they could be left behind for the use of Juan and other community workers. In Ometepe that year a team of intelligent British students – four of them from the same Christian Union at Birmingham University – forged some remarkable friendships with a group of unschooled Nicaraguan *campesinos*, farmers and fishermen.

The third team went to Bluefields on the Atlantic coast. Mike had taken note of the overcrowded and dilapidated classrooms in a church school there started five years earlier. The 134 pupils already served would increase in number as a grade was added every year. The school was threatened with eviction if it failed to meet a hefty rent increase, so the possibility of premises, on the site where STEP had earlier built their pig-barn, appeared to Ed and his wife Ligia an answer to their prayers. But there were few, if any, architects in Bluefields. 'What about that young lad Barnie, with the team last year? He say he was studyin' for architect. Couldn't he do the design, Mike?' suggested Ed with his customary cheerfulness.

Barnaby Hewitt swallowed hard when Nick passed on Ed's suggestion by phone. 'A pig-pen is one thing. Three classroom blocks plus offices and washrooms is something else. I'm only in my second year, man!' came the somewhat faint reply. Nick was not going to give up that easily. 'Have a word with your lecturers. They set you assignments to design great buildings on paper. Don't you think they'd be delighted you actually have the chance of constructing one? Why not make Bluefields your university dissertation?' This was an idea right at the heart of STEP's objectives: to give young people opportunities to extend their skills and wills. Time and again Steppers, initially diffident, had risen to bear substantial responsibilities and achieve great things. Finding a qualified architect to go out to Bluefields would have missed the point. Barnie rose to the challenge. He recruited Juliet Davis, a student at Cambridge, and they were joined by Laura Chudley from Sheffield University. Three second-year student architects designed and directed the construction of the rural classroom block at Bluefields.

Not all Steppers were young. The *South Avon Mercury*, under the headline 'GRANDAD OLDEST CHARITY VOLUNTEER YET TO NICARAGUA', reported how John Green, sixty-two, a recently retired engineer from Nailsea, had willingly headed out to the mud and mosquitoes of the jungle. He had contracted malaria there, but once back home, undeterred by this experience, had surged forward raising funds some months later so as to go back with the hovercraft.

On his STEP supervisory visits later that year Mike took the temperature of the 'fever' in Nicaragua. In August he met the President of the National Assembly, the Minister of Health and the Minister of Foreign Affairs all in one day. Dr Rachel Pinniger, who had more than twenty years' experience of the medicine of poverty, particularly in Bhutan and Nepal, accompanied him to the Ministry of Health. She had been with Mike in Papua New Guinea and had been persuaded to take time from her relief work in Ethiopia to investigate the health needs of south-east Nicaragua. The Minister was highly positive about the role that hovercraft might play, her vision even going further than Mike, for the moment, was able to follow: 'Couldn't you have a mobile operating table installed for emergency surgery in the remoter areas?' she asked.

As for the Tipitapa road, Mike found it badly deteriorated, and judged the prospects for the overland section 'poor'. But he was later to be taken aback when, mentioning his concerns casually at a meeting with Pablo Vijil, the Minister for Construction and Transport, the Minister promised to send a fleet of scrapers and earthmovers to 're-grade' the surface! Mike was suitably appreciative of this extraordinary offer, but on reflection wondered whether it was no more than an example of characteristic Latin panache. Time would tell.

On the final evening he was able to talk with Señor Antonio Lacayo, the Minister of the Presidency (Prime Minister). His wife Cristiana Chamorro – doña Violeta's daughter no less – was beside him. In 1991 she had retraced the steps of a journey to Greytown that her father had undertaken. 'Twenty years have passed,' she said pensively, 'but the questions he raised in *The Naked Feet* remain unanswered.' She was as interested as her mother in the project's attempts to address the matter.

At the same dinner table was a young British MP, Michael Watson, on a fact-finding visit as part of his shadow overseas aid brief for the Labour Party. He immediately offered his support. Mike had to smile as he shared with this likeable Scotsman, the socialist Member for Glasgow East, that the expedition's co-patron was a Conservative MP. Ted Heath had been patron of an earlier expedition. It had been Peter Dixon's idea. 'There's a link with adventure on water,' he had suggested, 'through his well-known passion for sailing. He was also Britain's representative on the Brandt Commission studying the world's North–South divide.'

'No problem,' Michael Watson replied, 'I admire Ted very much. Party politics aside I share common ground with him on many issues.' His help was practical and immediate: he offered to host a reception in the House of Commons! Potential supporters could be invited to the Jubilee Room beside the Great Hall of Westminster. Mike's mind immediately raced ahead. Might there be access to the terrace overlooking the Thames, so that the hovercraft themselves could put in an appearance? The occasion could be timed to coincide with the centenary of Britain's formal handing over of the Mosquito Shore to Nicaragua in 1894, and mutual statements of government goodwill could be exchanged. The two Michaels agreed to meet in the UK to develop plans further.

Getting back, Mike learnt that Shell UK had decided against the funding application. The proposals had been debated long and hard but it was considered inappropriate to make such an overseas grant when the company was on the verge of announcing widespread redundancies in the UK. Bad for public relations! The decision was a major blow and, as with Heathcote-Amory's promotion, frustrating that the search for funding should be hampered by factors totally beyond Mike's control. But a dark cloud proved to have a lighter, if not a silver, lining. The Shell official who had sought to help us had a Christian friend who offered to print a coloured brochure free of charge.

There was now another volunteer in the London office with Nick. David Coates had arrived fresh from Bluefields, and not in the best of health. He had been hospitalised in Bluefields with dengue when leading a STEP team there, and this highly unpleasant illness was compounded by a painfully infected arm from a contaminated drip. 'So what is it about Bluefields that makes guys like you and John Green want to go back?'

41

queried Nick. 'It's the people,' came the unhesitating reply. 'I was standing with Ed one day overlooking the rooftops of Bluefields – and thinking frankly how grubby and messy it all looked – when I asked him what he saw. He said quite simply: "I see the kingdom of God, David. What do you see?" That's why I want to go back, Nick. Because of people like Ed who look behind the visible and beyond the difficult; people who see the potential of lives rebuilt, strong in the strength and purposes of God.'

David's father had been the head teacher at Monkton Combe a Junior School when Nick was a pupil there. The fathers – like their lads – became friends, and Mike was often given the opportunity to talk to the school about 'adventure with a purpose'. One year he even took a hovercraft to the sports day! Three other young team members had been to Monkton at some time or other (Alan Blake, Chris Evans and Matthew Dixon), and the River Rover design team had schooled there too. Others came to joke light-heartedly about this 'Monkton Mafia'. Such a sizeable group from the same background might have resulted from no more than an 'old boy network' – it could hardly have been coincidental – but it may also have been a natural outflow from Monkton's original *raison d'être*. It was founded a hundred or more years ago as a school for the sons of British missionaries.

After Shell's disappointing news much depended, very much, on getting an ODA grant. David, Mike, Nick and Sarah (via a fax link with Managua) worked solidly for a month, between their other duties, to complete a comprehensive application to the ODA. The project fitted the general criteria well enough, but there was a large gap between the hands-on experience of these Third World volunteers and the development-speak called for in the application papers. Aware that most NGOs (Non-Governmental Organisations) competing for the available money had a plethora of development consultants at their service, the amateurs toiled to fit their deep commitment and surprisingly wide experience with jargon-ridden questions about 'assessing the environmental impact', the level of 'local empowerment' and the importance of 'sustainability'. Their completed thirty-page document included detailed annexes and a three-year budget, ambitious but realistic, totalling close to £1 million.

Meanwhile, the construction of River Rover 501 was being paid for with funds raised personally by team members. The attitude of Land Rover's project development manager at Solihull was 'if it's a machine, we can stick a Land Rover engine in it.' He had been pioneering new uses for his new power unit, from fire-trucks in Thailand to park buggies at Euro-Disney. So he had to be enthusiastic about it going into the River Rover! The company readily donated a Gemini III engine, their very latest version which was then still to be fitted to the 'Discovery' vehicle.

Griffon Hovercraft were going the second mile by starting to manufacture a 2000 TDX without requiring a further deposit. Thanks to a relatively full order book they were able to pencil 'Nicaragua' on it and allow us more time for fundraising. They invited us to a hovercraft fly-past at Gosport on 6 October to celebrate the eightieth birthday of Sir Christopher Cockerell, who invented them. Nick reported the occasion.

> The bracing sea-breeze off the Solent blew from our minds all thoughts of the ODA proposal. About a dozen of us, and a large crowd of other enthusiasts, stood on the slipway at the naval base scanning the horizon for a first sight of the flotilla. A glint of reflected sunshine marked a small helicopter above the outline of the leading craft. Rapidly some nine machines came into view speeding towards us across the estuary. At the head was a Griffon 2000 TDX in high-visibility colours 'That one's for the Brazilians,' said their marketing manager beside me. 'They want it for emergency rescue and patrol on Rio bay, just off the end of the airport runway.' Next came two more in camouflage; the marines used them for arctic exercises in Scandinavia. Behind were several larger craft with Sir Christopher himself at the helm of one and, snapping at their skirts and just visible, two River Rovers. And one of them was ours.

John Gifford, the vastly experienced Griffon engineer, hurled the leading machine up the steep slipway and flew it with great style across the road into the naval compound. When we turned our attention to the water again we realised that one River Rover had failed to arrive. The news reached us later that our craft had suffered a malfunction of a temperature gauge, a minor hitch, we were assured, of a kind not unexpected with a new engine installation. Though that was true, we came to consider it, in retrospect, a first sign of the problems that lay ahead.

A week later Mike was back on the Solent, this time inside one of the Griffons, with the Nicaraguan Minister of Transport beside him. Minister Vijil (who had pledged to level the Tipitapa road) had decided to flag Britain when returning to Nicaragua from the continent. They sped past at forty knots over a calm sea, taking it in turn at the controls. He went away with the highest expectations of the Griffon on the San Juan.

News from John Culver confirmed that 20 November was the exact centenary of 'the Mosquito Shore's re-incorporation to Nicaraguan sovereignty'. Mike arranged with Michael Watson, MP, to book the House of Commons room for the nearest week-day available. Wednesday, 23 November, was confirmed, and John Culver reported that the Nicaraguan Minister of Tourism would be present in official representation of his government. Every team member submitted names of their most significant commercial or media contacts. As the Jubilee Room could only accommodate seventy, every invitation had to count, and a highly selective guest list was drawn up. Harold Briley lobbied his political and media contacts, and even suggested to the PM's press secretary that John Major might like to look out of his office window at 1.30 to see the hovercraft on the river.

There were two River Rovers available for the day, one would be ours, and at Griffon's suggestion Texaco UK sent a Griffon of their own. Nick recalled his rowing days, when the racing eight had frequently been swamped by the wash of the most sedate river launches, and wondered whether speed restrictions on the river would detract from a spectacular hovercraft display. 'Don't worry,' said the Texaco pilot with enthusiasm, 'there's no speed limit as such; it's all dictated by the amount of wash you produce. As hovercraft produce next to none we shall go as fast as we like!' When Nick passed that on to Mike, they decided that what was good for the banks of the Thames must be good – ecologically speaking – for the banks of the San Juan.

The finale for the Jubilee Room event was already assured; a focus for the presentation itself was still required. A deft stroke of lateral thinking on Mike's part supplied an ideal solution. A year previously, he had suggested that Stan Baldock might like to do a portrait of Ted Heath, patron of the project. Sir Edward readily agreed, and invited Stan to several sittings at his home in Salisbury. Mike decided to unveil the finished portrait at the House of Commons, hoping one of the guests might persuade his company to purchase it for their boardroom!

On the day, most team members made themselves scarce by waiting on the riverside terrace, so as to maximise the space available in the Jubilee Room. In the event, it was difficult to move around among the ninety guests who crowded in. 'The President of the Republic of Nicaragua, Señora Violeta Barrios de Chamorro, has honoured me with the task of bringing her special greetings to Her Majesty, Queen Elizabeth II, to Her Majesty's Government, and to the people of Great Britain,' began Fernando Guzmán, the Minister of Tourism, with suitable diplomatic aplomb. 'The British Hovercraft Project is not just about travelling up a river that other British generations once navigated. It is about people like Squadron Leader Michael Cole and his team of volunteers providing humanitarian aid and development.' With Sir Edward unable to attend, Michael Watson returned the greetings of the Nicaraguan Government, not without a joke about the incongruity of a Labour MP standing in for the Tory Father of the House. Mrs Guzmán unveiled Sir Edward's portrait, and Mike, fully aware of the importance of the occasion, tried to make every word of his audio-visual count. The display on the river proved an exhilarating finale, with John Gifford in the Griffon spinning the forty-foot machine with consummate skill at the foot of Big Ben. 'Like a killer whale,' suggested Nick to his father, unaware in his excitement of anything inappropriate about the simile.

But Mike's eyes were on the crowded terrace. 'The real significance of the day,' he said with conviction, 'is not the money we may have raised, but this crowd of young people making their commitment before the demanding and – let's admit it, in some cases – cynical gaze of the public.'

In the following weeks, as the excitement died down, team members waited expectantly for responses from those they had invited to the House of Commons. No sizeable help materialised, though a spatter of what Mike liked to call 'mercy drops' fell steadily on the project office, enabling some £10,000 to be sent to Griffon before Christmas. Time was running out fast for the Griffon 2000 TDX. As the holiday approached, the firm explained that the construction had reached the point where the customer was required to specify cabin design. In the friendliest way possible they explained that other clients were showing an interest, and as they might not choose the tropical specifications that Mike was looking for, 'a serious injection of capital' (as bank managers are apt to call it) was now required if our name was to stay on the model under construction.

Mike turned again to the ODA for an early initial response to the proposal, and a letter from them arrived on Christmas Eve: 'I have now received some feedback from advisers in respect of the Hovercraft Communications project to Nicaragua and am sorry to say that the prospects for support under the Joint Funding Scheme look to be rather slim.' The wording was polite but, to most of us, fairly grim. A string of probable objections included the use of untrained volunteers, STEP project sustainability, and the high capital cost of hovercraft contributing to a very large budget for a 'first-time applicant'. Neither the project's considerable political support nor the likelihood of commercial benefits to Britain was mentioned. At home Mike looked across at the wooden carving of a Nicaraguan peasant farmer which stood by the family

Christmas tree; it had been a personal gift from Tourist Minister Guzmán. Inevitably the figure was barefoot. Mike knew that nothing could be done before the New Year. But what then? How could he raise 50 per cent of the Griffon's cost in order to keep the construction going? Was eighteen months' hard work to be wasted? Was a pair of shoes for the 'naked feet' to prove beyond our grasp?

Mike was now shouldering, largely alone, no small burden of responsibility. He continued to encourage himself with the immense amount of enthusiasm evident in Nicaragua. Said one team member with a wry sense of humour: 'There may be hover fever in Nicaragua; but it's a cold sweat in the UK!'

Chapter 5

Taking Risks

Mike was enjoying Boxing Day football on the radio when, not without some impatience, he was obliged to answer the phone. A supporter, asking for an update, got a picture of the unpromising financial situation. Unless the ODA responded with an unprecedented degree of speed we were going to need nearly £100,000 of bridging finance to keep the project alive. The caller said quietly: 'Leave it with me for a day or two, Mike. I've been approached by someone who may be able to help. I'll get back to you.' Two or three days later he did so, with the astonishing news that a young banker in the City had offered to make available to the project a loan of £90,000 interest-free, the money to be available later that week. Mike was staggered and humbled. He had gone through all his own ideas and had been forced back upon the promises of God alone. Now God had touched the life of a Christian high-flier, and his supportive wife, to release for God's purposes some of the wealth their gifts and talents had generated. The caller reminded Mike of a hymn, now somewhat out of fashion:

> When we have exhausted our store of endurance,
> when our strength has failed ere the day is half done,
> when we reach the end of our hoarded resources
> our Father's full giving is only begun.

Mike phoned the remarkable news to Griffon and, reinvigorated, was able to read the ODA letter in a new light.

He would grasp the handhold offered in its final sentence
– the opportunity to meet with a desk officer for further
discussion.

But he was frustrated. The Joint Funding Scheme claimed
to welcome innovative projects in emerging democracies, yet
their development model seemed to him to be 'set in concrete'.
His involvement in the voluntary sector went back to the time
when, more than twenty years before, he had chartered a
civilian Hercules 130 to deliver a Tear Fund water-drilling rig
to famine-stricken Ethiopia. In terms of the tactical operation
he felt his track record spoke for itself. What had niggled him
most was the ODA's objection to his using British volunteers
instead of employing local labour. STEP had repeatedly proved
that a group of Anglo-Saxon youngsters working on manual,
and sometimes menial, tasks, beside their Latin counterparts
could produce results that the more official model would find
impossible to match.

The west is obsessed with material prosperity. The rich
have arrived, the poor have been left behind, so development
projects major on improving material benefits, the be-all and
end-all of development! But in any decent English dictionary
the definitions begin with 'to unfold, reveal, bring from a latent
to an active and visible state'. In the photographic darkroom,
development brings hidden images to light. The lives of Third
World people are not as blank as may be imagined; there
are unseen images etched there. Unschooled, unskilled and
'un-rich' they may be, but God has folded up possibilities
within them. Unfolding such potentials was something that
Mike had watched over the years as teams had worked
side by side. New skills and values had often been learnt,
initiatives taken and new attitudes adopted, by British as well
as by Latin team members. He considered that that was an
important and worthwhile aspect of 'development', but was
not over-optimistic that the ODA would be able to appreciate
the point.

Meanwhile the hard graft of individual fundraising continued and Mike supported it wherever he found it. He
scraped ice off his windscreen early in January and drove

through sleet and hail to get to Reigate. Rob Case-Green, a modern languages and business student, was shortly to put his Spanish to good use in Managua, and had hired the Town Hall and laid on a selection of Latin food for a public presentation. Unfortunately, the weather meant that only a handful turned up. Mike consoled himself with two satisfying thoughts: if every 'hovercrafter' showed this sort of initiative the project would be assured and, second, he was glad that in crossing the country himself on such a night he had set the right example!

At a team briefing it was announced that the project would be renting a chalet in a relatively well-to-do area of Managua to provide some basic conveniences and, more importantly, some security from the threat of street crime, endemic in most Latin American cities. Some team members, remembering the very basic level at which they had lived when on STEP projects, showed some surprise. But Mike wanted a secure base. 'We shall need a bolt hole for rest and refreshment, especially for those who fall sick, as some will. The expedition itself will be exacting enough, I promise you. What's more, I'm envisaging that a group of UK supporters will be joining us for a few days. By the time we've crammed in masses of equipment and you lot are sleeping all over the floor, it'll be far from luxurious!'

'Dennis Smith and his wife Brenda, a qualified nurse, will be in Managua as house parents. They will help the STEP teams with their paper work and see them off up country. The STEP projects this year are particularly important. It may look to the country's poor as if the hovercraft is no more than a piece of high-profile, high-tech equipment which has nothing to offer them personally. We shall be able to point them to the school on the hillside above Bluefields, and to the vocational centre at Nueva Guinea. Incidentally, some of the Steppers are no more than school-leavers, but I want no prima donnas on the hovercraft, no 'them and us' mentality. We're in this together.

'Now about the hovercraft itself. There are three phases to the project. In May we attempt the journey to link the Atlantic coast with the capital city. The start at Bluefields will coincide with the official inauguration of the school. The craft, with as many on board as possible, will then travel down the coast to Greytown and on up the rapids and shallows of the San Juan river to El Castillo, where the Nicaraguans are planning a formal welcome. After calling at the old colonial city of Granada we shall attempt to cross the dry river bed northwards at Tipitapa to break through to Lake Managua and the capital, where the Mayor has promised to greet us with the keys of the city. We'll not rush it. Let's give the communities *en route* time to see the craft – and maybe take a ride in it. I anticipate the journey will take three to four weeks. That's phase one.

'During phase two we prepare a regular route along the San Juan by constructing maintenance and supply bases at strategic locations. During July and August we start building a lodge at Greytown and a base at Bluefields from where we shall be able to explore the neighbouring river systems. Your part? You fly out at the end of April. Those with limited time available will be back mid-June, and a top-up team of students has been recruited to replace you. Phase two ends in early September.

'Phase three is consolidation and extension and will operate with fewer, though hopefully more permanent, personnel. But to talk of that is premature. First the craft must prove themselves. Talking of craft, we have to get them to Nicaragua. Michael, over to you.'

Michael Pinkess put on his half-moon spectacles and opened his shipping file. He was clearly a Michael rather than a Mike! For most of his distinguished career he had gone to the City with the traditional bowler hat. Mike had been trying to get insurance for the Nepal project when first he met him. Hovercraft were then still a novelty; nobody knew if they were classified air or naval. Since they were controlled in the UK by the Civil Aviation Authority, Bowring got their aviation division to write the policy, thus involving Michael. Over the years he came to enjoy the hovercraft business as a welcome diversion from the rough and tumble of negotiating the big airline contracts. The two men got on well together, especially

51

when they unearthed their shared Christian commitment. As the friendship developed, Bowring Aviation not only provided cover for the hovercraft projects but generously agreed to pay each premium! In 1992 Michael took early retirement, so Mike challenged him to join the Papua New Guinea team in person. The Fly River delta was a world apart from the Square Mile, but Michael discovered the Gogodala tribespeople were in every sense a match for the shrewdest City negotiators. He loved it and was now eager for more of the same in Nicaragua.

Given his background in international transportation, he had accepted the task of making the shipping arrangements and had come up against a problem. Only a very few small coasters make scheduled visits to the Atlantic coast of Nicaragua, and using them would entail transhipment with all the associated extra costs and possibility of delay. The German firm Hapag-Lloyd had quoted for the alternative route of Felixstowe, Antwerp, through the canal, then northwards to Corinto on the Pacific seaboard. It was a wonderful illustration of just how inadequate are the shipping facilities in eastern Nicaragua. In order to import two forty-foot containers – hardly a major shipping operation – we were obliged to go an extra 300 miles south, pay unnecessary tolls through the canal, then add a further 800 miles north. As this would put the craft in the west, when we wanted them in the east, the idea of reversing the planned project was mooted, with the cross-country journey starting in Managua and finishing east in Bluefields. But the impact would have been greatly reduced and John Culver argued strongly against it. So Hapag-Lloyd and the long way round it had to be. And having got the containers to Corinto they would have to be hauled back 300 miles to the east, most of the way over bone-shattering roads, in order to get the craft to their starting point. Michael concluded: 'The voyage normally takes a month, so we shall need to load in late March to catch the April sailing.'

Mike finished the briefing with a challenge to prayer. He had heard a sermon on the previous Sunday highlighting the 'outrageous promises' of God to his people. 'Can we all believe that these extravagant assurances are for us?'

* * * * *

'Listen, I do understand your motivation,' croaked the ODA officer. He was far from well, but had postponed his meeting with Mike once already and was determined not to do so again. 'I made a personal contribution to a young person in my church who went on one of your projects two years ago,' he continued. 'My role now is to help you understand the criteria for joint funding.' Mike thought he detected, even in the flu-clouded eyes, a ray of hope. He listened, made notes, and when he left felt that it had been more encouraging than the previous correspondence. In particular, he was glad that the person handling the papers was sympathetic to the project's ethos.

Five days later Mike left for the final recce in Nicaragua accompanied by Gareth Smith. To call Gareth a double-glazing fitter from Devon, though a statement of fact, is akin to describing Indiana Jones as a lecturer in archaeology. Gareth fits windows to live, but lives for adventure, especially for Mike's variety of 'adventure with a purpose'. He had been one of the main hovercraft mechanics in Papua New Guinea, where he had gone with his equally enterprising wife Jenny. Having seen them at work, Mike challenged them to go to Nicaragua and to consider a longer commitment so that the project could move forward after its initial phases. So Gareth went with him on a final recce in order to get a 'hands-on' assessment of the situation before committing himself.

While Mike and Sarah launched into an exhaustive round of meetings with business and political leaders in Managua, Gareth and Matthew Falkiner set about determining how much fuel to lay down along the route and where to put it. Matthew was another ex-Stepper who had got back in touch, anxious to offer his skills elsewhere. As a recently qualified architect he had already met frustration in some of the projects he had worked on. 'It was supposed to be a prestigious shopping centre,' he complained, 'but there was no disguising the fact that it was a bull-ring. Why on earth would the Chinese want a bull-ring in Beijing?' It was a welcome offer. He could take over the Bluefields work now the three students were back at their desks. He could also design some hover garages.

The Managua enthusiasm quickly surfaced again. Shell confirmed 10,000 gallons of free diesel, an offer strangely matched by Pepsi's 10,000 bottles of soft drink! 'We now have essential intake for both men and machines,' faxed Mike to London. Texaco came up with a major offer of sponsorship the following day which Mike, having already committed himself to Shell, very reluctantly had to decline.

In Managua they were finalising plans for the hovercraft journey itself when the phone rang. It was the British Embassy to say that the President's office had just informed them that doña Violeta would like to meet the hovercraft and team personally in El Castillo, and the suggested date was the last Saturday in May. Mike's spirit soared as he realised that such recognition at the highest possible level in Nicaragua would surely enhance the project's credibility in the eyes of the ODA. He felt the need to fax London immediately: 'We now have a major state occasion on our hands. Please ask John Gifford – the world's number-one hovercraft pilot – if he will undertake to come out and drive the President.'

Back in the UK Dick Bell was able to test drive 'our' Griffon and was delighted with the wide range of improvements which had been added to the prototype used in China. Iain Morris, with training in graphic design, suggested the livery. Having the vehicle at our disposal was a remarkable privilege when it was but half paid for and the customer was quite unable to say when the balance would be forthcoming. John Gifford had agreed to release the craft, trusting Mike to produce the balance when it became available, on the basis of his having raised the money successfully in the case of China. 'But I wouldn't have done it for anybody else,' he added.

It was one thing to inspire such confidence, but quite another to set about honouring it. Mike wrote to two Christian Trusts who had supported his earlier work, asking them to consider making a £100,000 loan available for one year. John Culver supported the request by underlining the level of expectation in Nicaragua. Such a loan would keep the project going until the ODA grant became available later. Staff in the office worked hard on a supplement to the ODA document, which was almost as long as the original.

Meanwhile Sarah Lister was interviewed for an hour on prime-time TV in Managua. Not unnaturally, she found this high-profile occasion something of an ordeal, especially when it turned out to be a live phone-in. But she committed herself brilliantly and also dealt firmly with several guys who, having seen this good-looking blonde foreigner on the small screen, were obviously angling for rather more than hovercraft information when they phoned her after the show!

Brenda Muckley, like David Coates, is a member of All Souls Church, Langham Place, London. She had persuaded her boss at Times Newspapers to make plans for a special report when the project got under way. 'The way it works,' she explained to Mike, 'is that we sell as much advertising space as we can, and you get the same amount of space for your features.' So the team worked through their files and business cards in search of likely advertisers. Mike also took the opportunity of clarifying a point or two with her boss. 'If the features are going to have that negative or cynical tone that the press so often adopts when reporting Christians in the Third World, then don't bother.' The features editor thought the subject 'interesting enough without scratching around for sceptical jibes'.

Spitfire Quay, Southampton, on 22 March was the occasion towards which the team was now frantically working. The containers had been booked and Alan Blake had been appointed 'quartermaster', with the task of matching up the streams of requests arriving from Nicaragua with possible sources of supply in Britain. As the hovercraft were not going to fill both containers completely, and freight is charged by volume rather than weight, it provided a unique opportunity to take to Nicaragua whatever could be found that Nicaragua might need. Such was the variety of requests and procurements that Alan came to think of himself as organising a bizarre and gigantic boot sale, not least when the British Ambassador sent an urgent request on behalf of the MCC. A new set of stumps and some bats were wanted by the Managua Cricket Club. The MCC wanted new cricket gear! And Ray Pinniger, who perhaps was being starved of the sea in Ethiopia, asked if there would be room for her surfboard!

But ten days before loading, the River Rover crew punctured the growing excitement by reporting that the drive shaft of the 501 had failed on its final trials on Chase Water near Birmingham. The despondent engineers had taken it back to the workshop area of British Aerospace at Filton, kindly made available to them some weeks previously. They had bounced back and were working long hours to make the repairs in time for loading. And an enlargement was being planned to the thrust fan, a modification aimed at the core problem of transferring power from the lively Land Rover engine. But there was now no time for such major changes before shipping; the job would have to be completed, and tested, in Nicaragua. Mike realised the implications. He had asked for a maximum of sixty hours' water testing prior to accepting the craft. 'The President of Nicaragua will be viewing an untested hovercraft,' he complained. 'The whole thing is hugely unsatisfactory.' Stifling his more characteristic optimism, he had to admit to himself that the River Rover's contribution, barring a miracle, was going to be minimal.

Team members had gathered early outside the Griffon premises on Spitfire Quay when a 'Tautliner' drew up and the driver pulled back the side curtain to reveal masses of polythene-wrapped cartons. 'I'm told these are all for you,' he announced with cheerful finality. Alan Blake shrugged in some perplexity. A friend of his at Norton Health Care had remarked offhandedly that he could perhaps persuade the company to contribute a few drugs. 'They have a consignment nearing sell-by date,' he had later reported, 'mostly aspirin and paracetamol, prepared in 1990 for export to China. It was never delivered because of the fall-out over Tiananmen Square. They say we can have all 300 units.' He thought at the time that that meant 300 bottles of, say, 1,000 pills each – 300,000 had sounded a useful quantity. Alan now realised that it was much, much more. In trying later to make up an inventory, he was to calculate that we seemed to be taking enough headache pills for every man, woman and child in Nicaragua! There were other drugs, in relatively small quantities; some antibiotics and folic acid for the care of expectant mothers. With the driver anxious to get away, how was he to unload quickly such a quantity? The loan of pallets and a fork-lift truck from the Griffon stores brought him the answer.

Another major consignment arrived from Dublin. It was food. Peter Dixon had applied, as on other hovercraft expeditions, for short-shelf-life 'compo' from RAF stores. But large quantities of older stock had been taken out to the Gulf, in expectation of a much longer war, and it had been found cheaper to leave it in the desert than to drag it all back to the UK! So with tinned food scarce and expensive in Nicaragua, David Coates had doggedly phoned round the supermarkets to see what he could get. The result was that Marks and Spencer had offered some surplus stock. The price was knock-down, the quality satisfactory, but the menu somewhat limited and not best suited to the tropics: 1,500 tins of beef curry and 1,500 tins of *chilli con carne*!

All possible lines of enquiry to get a four-wheel-drive from a commercial sponsor had drawn a blank. And then, with no fuss at all, Gareth and Jenny Smith – who live a modest lifestyle – had quietly offered their most precious possession, their customised Land Rover. No formal contract was involved; they simply packed up, saw their vehicle into the container, and gave themselves and it to Nicaragua for as long as God should indicate. To Mike it was total commitment and he warmed to it.

Each arriving team member's car disgorged a further motley assortment of items to add to the growing mountain on the quay. With the Managua property largely unfurnished, Mike had called for everyone to find whatever they could. Four divan beds came from a top hotel undergoing refurbishment in Bath, and there were chairs, benches and small tables. A director of Salt and Dukes, a Birmingham firm, deeply impressed with what the STEP programme had earlier done for his daughter, gave a generous quantity of good-quality kitchenware and crockery. T-shirts and mugs came from the National Trust, colourful umbrellas and sun hats from the Legal and General; a wheelbarrow, pickaxes, shovels and hand tools were donated by Wickes, a DIY store where a Stepper, doing a holiday job, had talked his boss into letting him have them; used clothes in black bin-liners, and boxes of school materials and toys came from supporting families, groups and churches countrywide.

Dennis brought, for free distribution, boxes of Spanish New Testaments from the Scripture Gift Mission in London and something he had been astonished to find, a quantity of Scriptures in Miskito, the indigenous language of the Mosquito Coast. SGM staff were as delighted as he that these could be put to good use. Also a generous assignment of study books in English was donated by the charity Bookaid for use in Christian training centres on the English-speaking coast.

Alan knew well that the packing merited a plan, for the mountain was becoming large enough to challenge the available space. Furthermore, it was to be unloaded at different times and in different places. But what with the variety of unwieldly shapes and sizes, and the unpredictability of what else might arrive and when, he finally surrendered to the expedient of stuffing in whatever would go where: the River Rover, the Land Rover, the furniture, the bedding, the crockery, the tinned food, the Scriptures, the tools, the give-aways, the cricket gear for the MCC and, of course, the multi-million tablet consignment of analgesics. And there was room for Ray's surfboard too. It was with relief that, in the late afternoon, the first container was squeezed shut and the crane operator lifted it, at just over fourteen tonnes, onto a flat top. The engineers stayed on to load the Griffon into the second one the next day.

Iain Morris, who had been working as a comedy script writer, was briefed to organise a weekend of 'sponsorable' activities in the Lake District. He willingly turned from writing for BBC Radio's show *Weekending* to produce a racy promotional blurb. 'Coniston 95 will be gruelling but rewarding; tough but tender; and hard – yes, let's not beat about the bush, it'll be very hard. There will be a fourteen-mile race which starts and finishes in this delightful Lakeland village, the route taking a meandering circuit of Coniston Water. Unofficially it's for athletes in training, "wannabe" gladiators and people with good breathing technique. Alternatively you may walk up the Old Man of Coniston with a host of other Steppers, families, friends, dogs, complete strangers who happen to be there on the day and people from the road race who gave up after a couple of miles. You could clock up the miles on a bicycle or conceivably choose to swim the lake.' The style was not exactly Mike's, but he warmed to Iain's whole-hearted enthusiasm.

The annual race known as the Coniston 14 is now an official Amateur Athletic Association event which Steppers had attended since 1993 as a means of fundraising. The 'hovercrafters' now enthused some one hundred and fifty of their friends to take part. Twenty-five did the run, won by Jenny Brown of Birmingham University in the impressive time of one hour and thirty-five minutes. A much larger group braved icy fell conditions to reach the top of the Old Man. The most heavily sponsored participant was Willy, the Mitford-Slade family's golden retriever. Son Tim was joining the Nicaragua team as part of his year off before university. Friends had been persuaded to sponsor the family dog to the tune of £2,500. Señora Verónica Gómez, the new Nicaraguan Ambassador in London, sent two of her staff. In 1996, she and her husband were to slog over the fells themselves to raise money for the project.

At a final briefing on the Sunday Mike warned: 'There are unforeseen risks; problems will occur without warning. Your reaction will need to match each developing situation, your personal resolve be adequate for every circumstance.' Unforeseen risks? Mike was right. But none was facing more risk than he. If the ODA were to turn the project down, considerable resources of capital would have to be found from somewhere else in order to pay for the hover-craft and return the interest-free loan. Would God be able? Mike believed in taking risks; the Bible was full of people who did: Abraham, who followed God without knowing how it would end; David, who sized up Goliath and took a risk; Daniel, who took a certain risk with the mouths of lions.

So he closed the weekend with a prayer that God would work powerfully through the team in Nicaragua and an 'Amen. See you at Gatwick!'

Chapter 6

Frustrating Delay

'Hey Al, I'm sure glad we took those seats outta the RV,' chuckled the tall Texan to the shorter one, as they surveyed the team's luggage piled high on the trolley train at Houston International Airport. We walked out of the air-conditioning into a wall of heat and humidity. George enlightened us. 'An RV,' he explained, stabbing his finger at the gleaming fourteen-seater parked opposite, 'is a Recreational Vehicle.' George Bruner and Al Pessara of Tallowood Baptist Church, Houston, had become well known to us; since 1991, over a hundred of our travellers had been treated to overwhelmingly generous 'southern' hospitality when stopping over *en route* for Managua.

This support was the result of a link which already existed between Tallowood and Mike Cole's home church at Gorsley. On the face of it it seems an unlikely partnership; a mega-congregation of over four thousand in urban Houston, working out of a magnificent modern complex right on the buckle of the American Bible-belt, and a two-hundred-and-fifty-strong Baptist church in rural Herefordshire, which has been serving the local farming community for more than two centuries. Young people from Tallowood had visited Gorsley in 1988 for a Crossroads Mission to schoolchildren. Tallowood's kind care of Steppers in Houston was one of the many repercussions of that visit.

'Here, wear these,' said Al, upending a kitbag full of Tallowood basketball vests. 'We'll crank up the church washing machines, and you could give them after to the kids in

61

Nicaragua!' Al had spotted several of the team inspecting woefully the contents of their rucksacks. Back in Britain a thousand-jar consignment of jam and pickled onions, donated by Chivers Hartley, had arrived too late for the sea container, so the kind gift had been distributed through team members' luggage. They discovered it took only one smashed pickled-onion jar to impart the stench of vinegar to the entire contents of a kitbag. 'Phew! That should keep the mosquitoes at bay,' smirked one whose own kit was unaffected. It was no problem for Tallowood's 'Minister for Recreation'. Al bundled the stinking clothes off to the laundry and left the team to put their new shirts into action on the church's full-size basketball court.

'Minister of Recreation' may conjure up no more than the quaint picture of a village parson organising the PCC's annual cricket match, but for Al Pessara it means the full-time management of a large sports and activities complex comparable to the leisure centre of any UK town. For anything more than the normal packed programme of basketball leagues, aerobics, raquetball and the like, Al calls in his old fishing pal George Bruner as reinforcement.

Two of Tallowood's RVs, with George and Al at the wheel, had weaved the team through the ten-lane traffic of Houston's evening rush hour. A 'night on the church floor' proved to have a less demanding connotation than it would have had in Britain. Having struggled to finish a Texas-sized hamburger and fries, they stretched out comfortably in a room full of sofas and soft gym mats.

For Nick Cole jet lag struck long before dawn and he lay gazing up at the whirring ceiling fans, reflecting on the project's uneven fortunes over the previous fortnight. It was an opportunity to step back from the frantic activity and gain a balanced perspective; a brief stopover in a sort of no man's land, UK preparations now behind, Nicaraguan challenges still to come.

The departure of the two STEP teams from London on 13 April had lifted spirits because the major part of the project's work force was finally on its way: twenty-five willing volunteers, including the first two Steppers from Germany. As they had turned away from the departure gate at Gatwick Mike Cole had passed Nick an envelope. 'Please keep that confidential,' he said. 'I don't want a morale problem among the younger team members.' It was a chilling letter from the ODA informing us that our funding application had definitely been turned down. Typically, Mike was already focusing on how to move forward positively before Nick could even grasp the full impact of the shattering news. 'But by the same post I received good news from Sir Edward Heath,' he went on. 'He considers the project's potential "far exceeds the financial cost". Encouraging and helpful timing! I've sent copies to the PM's press secretary, the minister responsible at the Foreign Office, and the Under Secretary at the ODA.'

'What do I say to President Chamorro and her ministers?' mused Mike. 'Their meeting with us on the Rio San Juan on 27 May is a major Anglo-Nicaraguan occasion: "Your Excellency, we have opened a proven route to reach 90,000 of the poorest people of Nicaragua. British young people have worked hard to raise 50 per cent of the finance but alas the British Government has not provided the backing you had good reason to expect. I fear the Griffon hovercraft will now have to return to the UK." How would that sound? I've gone at them hard, but the ODA letter is thin.' Thin indeed. Nick's initial reaction had been anger. The letter merely repeated the criticisms levelled in their Christmas Eve communication. He felt like a schoolboy sent away to rewrite his essay because the question had not been answered. He shouted out aloud in his anger: 'But I did answer the question!' It might have been acceptable, if disappointing, to be told that there was not enough aid money to go round, but to be turned down again because they had not answered the question – frankly, he found that insulting.

'Calm down, Nick! It was never going to be easy to fit our innovative project into their rigid template. I'll pursue the political battle in prayer and down every other avenue. Ted Heath's support gives me renewed conviction that what we are attempting is worth fighting for.' Our patron, the former Prime Minister, was revealing an altruism that was at odds with the public caricature. A 'bitter, self-absorbed man, still tilting at his nemesis in the person of Lady Thatcher' was how *The Times* was later to describe him in an eightieth-birthday feature. It seems that once Sir Edward has decided that something is worthwhile he is immutable, whether in defying a referendum on a single European currency or struggling to help the poorest and remotest in Nicaragua. In Lord Hailsham's plain but endearing words: 'He's a pugnacious old bruiser.'

'For a start I shall have to delay my departure for Nicaragua until early May,' went on Mike. His decision to keep the negative ODA news confidential and shoulder alone the burden and responsibility of the resulting financial crisis unhappily resulted, at one point, in the Ambassador in Managua knowing more about the matter than the team's own field staff. But it was characteristic of him not to want to share bad news with the wider team until he had some positive progress with which to maintain morale.

Little could be done anyway over the Easter weekend. News of a further setback was waiting in the office on the Tuesday. A fax from Managua announced that the estimated arrival date for the containers had been put back from 3 to 12 May, due to docking congestion at ports of call *en route*. The extra week built in for contingencies had vanished. Any further delays and the programme would be under serious threat. Furthermore, with the advance party of engineers booked to leave the UK on 20 April and the main group a week later, there would now be an extended period in Managua while waiting for the containers.

On a much needed lighter note, a query by one young first-time Stepper was reported from Managua. Taking her leaflet on 'Health and Hygiene for Visits to Developing Countries' with commendable seriousness, she was heard to ask the day after arrival: 'Shouldn't we be showering in boiled water?'

In Tallowood Nick wandered over to the Coke machine in the foyer for an early-morning can. He reflected that maybe, in retrospect, the ill tide had started to turn a couple of days previously when KHD Deutz, manufacturers of the ever reliable diesel engine in the Griffon, had sent an impressive cheque as a discount on the engine, as well as a wide selection of free spares. That same day news arrived of a £1,000 discount on the shipping costs. Though not all the hoped-for help was coming from Britain, here at least was some Teutonic goodwill.

Another foreign firm had completed the day's hat trick. The staff in Managua had been looking for the gift or loan of a four-wheel-drive or pick-up truck for use during the project. Enquiries had drawn a complete blank until a cold call to Budget, the local franchise of an American car rental company, sparked some interest. A meeting followed which resulted in the immediate loan of a brand-new pick-up for runs to the airport, and a pledge of two older vehicles for the period of the expedition itself when countless journeys over rough roads would be involved. Sarah Lister had faxed triumphantly to London: 'Our new pick-up is sitting outside.'

This was the truck that whisked the party from Managua airport the next day. The airport's sweet smell of jet fuel receded in the hot night air only to be replaced by acrid diesel fumes and the stench of burning rubber. Rob Case-Green was driving: 'It's not just tyres braking,' he explained. 'Look! Striking workers burn old tyres here as a picket-line activity on the street. There's always some sort of demonstration going on.' The road ahead was partially blocked by a fire belching black smoke into the orange glow of the street lamps. Rob swerved to avoid the obstacle and drew up at the next set of traffic lights. A grimy grinning face pushed through the driver's door, followed by a grubby outstretched hand. 'The street kids are quite cheeky,' said Rob as he put a boiled sweet into the boy's fingers, from a stock carried for the purpose. 'He really wants money, of course.'

* * * * *

This was Managua, the capital. Nicaragua has had three capitals: first Granada, then León. The former was Catholic and conservative, the latter secular and liberal; and in the mid-nineteenth century the tension between the two became so great that Managua, then a sleepy town situated between them, was given the privilege, as it were by default.

Unfortunately subsequent history has shown that, for a capital, it hardly occupies the most felicitous of locations. Its centrality is strategic, but it stands on the southern shore of Lake Managua, a body of stagnant and heavily polluted water. Worse still, beneath the city there runs a major geological fault. Twice this century it has savagely made its presence felt and is always likely to do the same again.

But earth tremors and putrid lakes are not the only, or perhaps the most immediate, problems to be faced by visitors to this highly unusual city. Can there be anywhere another quite like it? If you ask Managuans where the city centre is, they will almost certainly say: 'We don't exactly have a city centre.' No high-rise modern blocks huddle together downtown, no concentrated shopping area, no cluster of banks or businesses. Managua has been described as a 'non-city'!

In part, the strangeness is a legacy of the geological fault. During Holy Week 1931, an earthquake destroyed thirty blocks and killed some 1400 people. Forty years later, just before Christmas 1972, the city was flattened again. This time 250 blocks of the centre were rased, some 6000 died, and 300,000 were left homeless. International aid poured into the country, but progress was paralysed by the corruption of the political regime and by uncertainties about rebuilding on so vulnerable a site. Then came the revolution and the war. The result is that today, all of twenty-five years later, a vast area of Managua is nothing but open grassland, punctuated by a few – very few – new buildings and by one or two ghostly ruins where twisted building iron towers upwards, and crags of misshapen concrete hang precariously down. Highways dissect the area, heading towards no immediately discernible destination.

So where do people shop? The poor go to sprawling and crowded open markets; the more affluent to small malls newly developed in residential areas. Banks, businesses and government offices spring up haphazardly along the highways; restaurants, travel agencies, small supermarkets, boutiques and other services nestle inconspicuously between the chalets of middle-class suburbia.

In Managua, whatever you are looking for is unlikely to be as readily identifiable as you would wish, and the problem of finding it will be complicated by the long-established custom of giving no names to the city's streets. Addresses are quoted by the particular district in which they are to be found, followed by a reference to any one of a series of recognised departure points across the city. So the Project house to which Rob was heading was in La Colonia (the district), one block 'up' from the Atlas Gymnasium (the point of departure) and thirty yards to the 'south'. As long as you know where the Atlas Gymnasium is – or it might be the Santa Ana church, the Metro Ciné, or the Shell filling station – and you can interpret correctly the 'ups' and the 'downs', and as long as you know which way is north, you should be able to find what you are looking for!

Unfortunately, not fully satisfied with this markedly unusual system, Managuans have added a further complication. *Arriba* (up) does not mean 'up the slope', and *abajo* (down) does not mean 'down the slope'. The lie of the land has nothing to do with it. 'Up' means 'east' and 'down' means 'west'. So you may be going uphill on the 'down' leg, and downhill on the 'up' leg. But that is not the end of it. You will discover that some places are still quoted as 'departure points' although they have long since ceased to exist. So you find yourself heading two blocks up from 'where the white tree used to be'! Newcomers are incredulous. Those who stay soon admit that somehow the system works. Fortunately, taxi drivers know every reference point in the city, whether they still exist or not, and can distinguish quickly between their 'ups' and their 'downs'.

Driving across the city is a risky and often breathtaking adventure. The city's poor lie in wait at all traffic lights: women with babies, the war-disabled and the 'street children', from the tenderest age up. Apart from hands stretched in through open windows, they are over your bonnet with bucket and squeegee, and have the windscreen cleaned before you can tell them that it was done at the last set of lights. Others hawk a vast variety of merchandise, none of which, except perhaps a newspaper, a foreigner is ever remotely likely to buy: sealed plastic bags of water, iced lollies, lottery tickets, lucky charms, chewing gum; or even something more substantial, like an electric fan perhaps, a set of garden furniture, or even a complete home-made exhaust system for your car! How a driver can haggle, strike a bargain, buy, drag it on board, pay and pocket the change, all before the lights turn green, will remain a mystery for most of us. Some evidently can!

Hundreds make a meagre living by carting items from one side of the city to the other on platforms mounted precariously on discarded car wheels. The better-off use horse or donkey, but many are one-manpower rickshaws laboriously pulled with hands, shoulders and even forehead.

Public transport varies from the respectable in up-market areas to make-shift trucks with detachable ladders for boarding and loose wooden benches for sitting; others offer only hanging-on room. Some taxis run predetermined routes with passengers sharing. But one way or another the resilience of Managuans allows them to move about their city at least as fast as Londoners are likely to move about theirs.

With few major buildings surviving the quake, there are few focal points. One exception would be the massive, Aztec-like nine-storey Intercontinental Hotel, used by dignitaries, businessmen and such international tourists as come. At the time of the quake, Howard Hughes, the multi-millionaire American recluse, was occupying the whole of the top floor, together with his sizeable retinue. The view, if he was calm enough to watch, which seems unlikely, must have been apocalyptic.

The old cathedral survives only as a shell, open to the sky. Weeds sprout in the aisles. A new building has recently been consecrated a couple of miles away. Prince Charles would be unlikely to approve. Most people think it exudes a Moorish, Middle-Eastern air. Sadly, in 1995 anyway, worshippers were paddling in inch-deep pools under a badly leaking roof!

This has always been an agricultural country. Thomas Gage, an Englishman who visited the isthmus in the 17th century, writing in 1637, pronounced it 'the paradise of America, so fertile, so abundant in the fruits of the earth, a place of gardens and thriving trade'. But it is the urban population that grows fastest, Managua three times faster than anywhere else in the country. Because of natural disasters, and thousands still in exile, growth has not been quite as explosive as in many other Latin capitals, but an irrepressible human tide continues to flood city-wards. More than half the migrants from the countryside are minors in need of schooling. The result is a total overload of social services already starved by the country's general economic collapse.

Somehow, though unemployed and without benefits of any sort, people survive. DIY homes start as tin or cardboard shelters but gradually take shape as basic structures. Families gather whatever building materials they can, put them together, then wait for months or years in the hope that the house will one day be complete. Hope is the great virtue; without hope this city, like all Third World cities, would die.

The team were soon to experience first-hand the daily cuts in domestic and commercial supply of both water and electric power, for periods of up to five hours. The wealthy avoid the inconvenience by erecting water towers in their gardens, and by buying stand-by generators. With late-summer temperatures averaging 38 °C, team members were to think of the fan and the cold shower as two of life's simplest, but most indispensable, pleasures. The poor – the vast majority – of Managua, are denied both.

It is perhaps the water shortage that must frustrate them most, for the city is surrounded by water, and indeed the history of the whole country revolves around her lakes and rivers. Too much water in the east, where only the forgotten live, and too little in the west, where everything happens. Dr Jaime Incer, Nicaragua's most renowned geographer, has said: 'As Managua, overwhelmed with problems, goes without both light and water, and lives grudgingly beside a putrid lake, the river San Juan pours into the Atlantic every four minutes as much fresh water as the capital requires in twenty-four hours. Future development must look towards this water supply.'[1] So we came to see that opening up the river San Juan to provide 'shoes' for the 'naked feet' of the Atlantic coast might ultimately, however indirectly, do something too for those whose feet tread the streets of this hot and thirsty capital.

Yet though life remains a dire struggle for tens of thousands, there is little evidence of a renewal of revolutionary violence. Admittedly, silhouettes of Sandino, the earlier revolutionary, still stand against the skyline, and in the middle of the central wasteland a youth in bronze stands barebreasted on a pedestal, twice as large as life, both arms brandishing aloft an automatic rifle. But in practice the cost of war lies heavy on Nicaraguans; people yearn for a lasting peace and some evidence of economic progress, of daily life becoming less of a burden.

We were to learn that the resilience and warmth of Managuans enables them to be welcoming to strangers, grateful at the least sign of friendliness and, in the case of so many, seemingly happier than they have any right to be. Mindful of our affluent but largely dissatisfied Britain, coming to know this city was a humbling and enriching experience. The conviction grew upon us, if ever we had doubted it, that human joys are not closely related to earthly comforts. If they were, Managua would be a much sadder place than it is.

* * * * *

Rob got his passengers to headquarters. After eighteen months of preparation they found the arrival exhilarating. Managua's crowded clamour cut a striking contrast to the deserted sidewalks of downtown Houston, where people pass seamlessly from air-conditioned homes to air-conditioned destinations in air-conditioned cars.

Over a number of weeks a robust debate via fax had developed between Mike and the Managua staff about the use of 'spare' team members in Nicaragua during the period before the cross-isthmus journey could begin. Early on, Sarah had faxed for advice. She suggested forming work teams to do some needed decoration of earlier STEP constructions. Mike replied: 'The team will be fully occupied prior to the containers' arrival. Please don't commit them to fill-in duties. There's the Tipitapa section where they could usefully be employed for a month preparing the road for hauling the hovercraft overland.' He was tempted not to take entirely at face value the Minister of Transport's earlier promise that the road would be re-graded, and all his experience led him to preserve a contingency period. The Managua staff, encouraged by more recent meetings with the Minister's subordinates, were convinced that the team's help would not be much required, and continued to be concerned – not without some reason – about how to keep the team both happy and usefully occupied during the waiting period.

But Mike had other factors to consider. He was keenly aware that precious days of active expedition were slipping away from team members who had worked hard to raise funds, deferred college courses, arranged leave from work and, in some cases, even given up employment in order to participate. He could not allow them to mark time much longer in the UK; as many as possible had to be overseas by the beginning of May. He was well aware of the possibility of hold-ups – not least from the six-week delay he had suffered in China. So he was glad he had warned everyone to pack five good paperbacks. For himself he bought a copy of Margaret Thatcher's memoirs, sensing that both he and the team might need some of her resilience to cope as well with periods of unavoidable delay as they undoubtedly would with the intense challenges of the adventure itself.

Ken Pollard was a skilled builder; there was no difficulty in finding an immediate job for him. He went to Bluefields to help direct Steppers in construction work at the Verbo school. The target was to complete the first classroom block by 21 May, when Government ministers were expected at an opening ceremony planned to coincide with the arrival of the hovercraft at Bluefields. The 1994 STEP team had built the basic structure, but with less than a month to go an enormous amount of work remained to be done.

Ken had been a late recruit to the project. The Rev. Lawrence Copley, the new minister at Ashby Wesley Methodist Church in the northern steel town of Scunthorpe, had needed some plumbing at the manse, and was advised that a self-employed builder named Ken generally did all maintenance work for the circuit. Over a tea break among a pile of radiator pipes, Lawrence soon uncovered Ken's keen interest in Christian mission overseas. He learnt that he had spent years in Africa teaching science in tough locations. On returning to England he had needed somewhere to live so had built from scratch a four-bedroom house for his family. 'How on earth did you manage that?' asked an astonished Lawrence. 'I read a book on it, read it again and then got on with it.'

Lawrence had heard enough. The fact that Ken and his son had also built, and now fly, their own light aircraft, was superfluous. 'You need to meet my friend Mike Cole,' he said. Over the years he had sent a stream of young people from his previous church to STEP projects. What had begun simply as kind support for his friend Mike's work overseas grew into a deep conviction. Lawrence had seen the Christian commitment of members of his congregation revolutionised by their STEP involvement. So he pointed the practical hands of this big but gentle man towards Nicaragua. From the first day Ken led by his personal example of unflagging hard work.

But others in Managua were now stuck, as if in a log jam. Some changed their priorities with a view to staying active. Painting at the Los Brasiles school, where two members put graphic design training to great effect, producing an imaginative scriptural mural, was a worthwhile job in itself, but the overriding value of the task was in occupying potentially restless team members.

Some minor activities were more closely linked to the expedition itself. A morning with pickaxes and shovels cleared the bank where the hovercraft would emerge from the Tipitapa river on to dry land. The skill of an agile local tenant farmer was remarkable. Looping a rope over the lower branches of the river-side trees and bending them to the ground, he catapulted himself fifteen feet or more into the air by releasing the boughs while holding on to the rope. Then, balancing with toes splayed on swaying branches, he hacked away the foliage with his machete so that they would clear the hovercraft's fans beneath.

Meanwhile Spanish-speaking members were chasing around government offices with forms in triplicate and passport photographs in quadruplicate to apply for charitable category visas for the party. Nick and Sarah battled through sporadic power cuts to draw up a funding application to the Texaco Foundation on computers that an American relief agency had kindly given them access to. Nick was still acclimatising to the heat. Splashes of sweat fell on to the keyboard as he realised he was soaked and his head was pounding.

Others occupied themselves in private tasks. Dr Ray Pinniger, who had barely paused in England *en route* from her medical work in Addis Ababa, wrestled with an overdue UK tax return. Others scribbled diaries or letters home, keeping the heat at bay with countless Pepsis. The company, true to its word, delivered the first month's free quota: 1,800 bottles in Managua and a similar number in Bluefields. Fortunately, warm Pepsi being predictably unappetising, they came with the loan of large fridges at each location. The fridge in the Managua kitchen, power cuts notwithstanding, proved a saving factor for those in charge of buying and preparing food too.

Team activities were organised, including a bizarre *boules* tournament played with heavy plastic balls unearthed from the bottom of someone's kitbag. A Saturday morning was spent in cricket practice with the local expatriates, although the new bats and gloves they had asked for were still, of course, on the way. But one could only enjoy reading, writing and team games for so long. After days of self-absorption, a blanket of lethargy, characterised by a disinclination to volunteer for the necessary domestic chores, fell across some. With thirty in the house, the most basic facilities were stretched to the limit and, given the daily cuts to power and water supply, sometimes beyond. Meals demanded everyone's co-operation and the degree of organisation the Smiths felt necessary probably seemed over the top to those affected by the general ennui.

On 7 May Mike Cole arrived and quickly took stock of the way team members were coping. He confided to Nick that he was going to have to draw on all his experience to hold together the team's wide range of individual interests. 'Other expeditions have been full of specialists; this time we have lots of young general-purpose volunteers, and I've got to ensure that they all find fulfilment in the project. I've also got to keep waging the financial battle which, out here, means controlling stringently the use of project funds. It's been a week since my last urgent request went to the British Government. I'll fax them today with the punchline: "I am now in Managua in very thin clothing".'

On 10 May came the highly unwelcome news that the *Vladimir* had been deferred a further three days. Mike reacted by dispatching team members in our pick-up to visit the school on the island of Ometepe in Lake Nicaragua, where a previous STEP team had worked. Sarah and Matthew were not entirely happy at having the Budget vehicle tied up in this way and there was some sympathy for their view, but Mike felt that he had to put available resources at the disposal of the whole team, getting everyone involved, even if it impaired efficiency in some way. So the truck went.

It was encouraging, after months of praying at home as individuals, to be able to pray together about the big issues: the funding, the arrival of the freight, team dynamics, the preparation of the Tipitapa road. Regarding the latter, there had been a standoff earlier in the week between the Ministry of Transport and the contractors, who felt they had not been properly paid for the last job. So we took it as a direct answer to prayer when Matthew announced that bulldozing had actually begun.

In devotions one day Dick Bell quoted a somewhat obscure Bible verse he had come across in Ecclesiastes. 'To the sinner God gives the task of gathering and storing up wealth, to hand it over to the one who pleases God' (Eccles. 2:26). 'So who knows,' said Dick, with a twinkle in his eye, 'where the Lord might be lining up the necessary cash?' Lack of British commercial interest in Nicaragua had made it difficult to find secular sponsors, and funds had so far been provided largely through Christians at home. Dick's comment gave rise to some debate on the scruples often attached to the funding of Christian projects. If, say, we were opposed to gambling, would we accept a grant from a lottery? Some Christians, probably a minority, argue that they would accept a gift from the devil himself, if there were no strings attached. Dick's verse gave some plausibility to that position. So the team began to wonder if we were to see God provide in some unusual and surprising way.

We made contact too with local Christians. Dennis, who had worked closely with Latin American Churches for many years, was keen to see the project's links with the Nicaraguan Church widened and strengthened. We were of course there at the request of local pastors, but given the growing strength of Nicaraguan Protestants, he judged that a project given such exposure in the national press demanded and deserved contact with church leaders at national level.

The growth of Latin American evangelicals during the past fifty years has been remarkable. A former literary editor of *The Guardian*,[2] has quoted a Belgian Catholic priest: 'They are growing overwhelmingly and at an ever-increasing rate . . . a tidal wave that nothing can stop.'

The team had heard that some 30 per cent of Nicaraguans were now active evangelicals, and realised that if this figure was true something extraordinary must have happened, for Latin American countries are still quoted as being 95 per cent or more Roman Catholic. But there was plenty of evidence to support the breathtaking swing towards the *evangélicos*. They were everywhere. When Brenda Smith went to buy fish on her first morning, and wanted to get the hang of the chaotic open market, it was quite easy to find a dependable market woman to give her some help. There she was, sitting behind her pile of pineapples reading the Bible, sure sign of an *evangélico*. Amazing attraction! Little schooling, poor in the things of the world, yet fascinated by the Word of God.

The team split across a number of local churches on the first Sunday morning. Dennis took a taxi at random, only to discover that the cabby was *en route* to his own all-age Sunday School too! The church Dennis chose met, as thousands meet across the world wherever the Church is growing, in what had once been a home in a residential area. More than a hundred Managuans, a cross-section of the social spectrum, sang and praised for an hour in the sweltering heat, then listened attentively to a forty-five-minute talk on the Sermon on the Mount. The pastor was apparently accustomed to having his work interrupted with comments and questions from the floor. Just as well, for the congregational participation was abundant and highly thought-provoking.

'You're telling us that it says here we ought to pray and fast in private – not on the street corners. So how come you announce publicly today we're going to have a special day of prayer and fasting on Friday?'

'Fasting's OK for people who have nothing else to do but pray. I have to work. Do I have to fast too?'

'You say we ought not to worry about tomorrow – about money, or what we shall eat or what we shall drink. I've worked hard for the little I've got, and I want my children to have a better chance than I've had. Is that wrong? In the States Christians believe in keeping a bank balance for the future. What do you say about that?'

Those who could understand but little of what was going on had to be impressed none the less with these lively exchanges. For his part Dennis was stimulated by the sincerity and depth of the questioning and by the pastor's ability to cope. How many ministers in Britain, he wondered, would do as well if publicly interrupted every Sunday? He thought it might be good for the Church if they were.

The following week he sought out the First Baptist Church where the pastor was a gifted Nicaraguan, Dr Gustavo Parajón, who had spent some years in the States. The singing was lively and the choir among the very best he had come across anywhere in Latin America. The well-crafted sermon was both biblical and holistic, not often the case among Latin American evangelicals. Many believe that involvement in social concerns is a diversion from the main task of 'saving souls'. Parajón was the man who had been influential in founding CEPAD,[3] which worked effectively after the devastating 1972 earthquake. It had broken down the deeply etched denominational barriers of Protestantism, mobilised aid to the thousands of victims and, for the very first time, brought the evangelical Church to the notice of the nation. When the revolution finally came, CEPAD stood firmly behind it. When, as many see it, the revolution was hijacked by the communists, churches were divided about supporting it. Because CEPAD stayed with the Sandinista line, some member organisations broke away and formed their own inter-church committee. It was the old left-wing, right-wing divide. Worse was to follow. Others tried to steer clear of both by forging groups they thought of as totally apolitical. And such is the patchwork quilt of socio-religious understanding – or misunderstanding! – which persists in an otherwise encouraging evangelical scene today. There are sharp personal memories, too, of unmentionable happenings during the civil war, which go on drip-feeding the bitternesses.

So to which group, if any, was the project to relate? It might have been thought wise as expatriates to 'go it alone', and stay clear of the political quagmire. But what had been planned had already excited the whole nation, and therefore had to be of interest to the whole Church. It was no flash-in-the-pan expedition to be packed up after three weeks and carted back to Britain. It was meant to produce a pair of shoes for the country's naked feet, something for Nicaragua to wear and to go on wearing. It was essential to involve as many Christian groupings as possible, while avoiding the party-political maelstrom on the one hand and the sad religious schisms on the other. Was that feasible?

Dennis learnt that it might be. Prejudices would keep some organisations away from anything promoted by CEPAD, and CEPAD would steer clear of anything promoted by 'the opposition'. But prominent church leaders on all sides were convinced – though not without indications of self-conscious embarrassment – that if a third party were to organise a meeting to explain the project, both camps would come! Leading figures still respected each other as individuals, though between the 'headed notepapers' antipathy remained!

Dennis made a mental note that if such a meeting ever came about something ought to be said about forgiveness and reconciliation. But then he reminded himself that Britain had not known the agony of civil war for over three hundred years. These Christians were growing strongly, had come so far, that finding splits among them made him sad. But he dared not be judgmental. They had gone down a Via Dolorosa it had never been his lot to travel.

For the moment more urgent tasks demanded attention. The ship was now to dock at 7 a.m. on Monday, 15 May, and would, we understood, begin to unload immediately. After so many delays, the group of four who drove across to Corinto, on the Pacific coast, early that morning decided that 'seeing would be believing'! So there was jubilation when, turning on to the dock area, the first thing they saw was the distinctive orange of a Hapag-Lloyd container moving away from the hull of the *Vladimir* on an articulated truck! The second was visible on deck, only third in line for unloading. Dick Bell flagged down the driver to see what was happening. We had a priceless letter authorising imports free of all customs charges, by decree of President Chamorro herself. Were the port gates to be flung open to allow the containers to be driven straight out?

Alas! Seeing was not to be believing. The truck turned into a huge caged compound where the first container was gently lifted to the ground. And so began the paperwork. Matthew Falkiner presented the letter of exemption only to discover that it should have been exchanged in Managua for an official certificate of *exoneración*. After lengthy discussion, it emerged that our papers specified we were bringing in a Land Rover. Due to a long-running dispute between the local agent and Land Rover in the UK, the Nicaraguan Government had placed an embargo on their import. The officials in Corinto were apparently struggling to come to terms with contradictory orders from above.

Matthew phoned through to the team house in Managua, and Sarah shouted down an impossibly faint line: 'Right, we'll make enquiries this end.' She launched into a long series of phone calls, polite but determined, and was passed from bureaucrat to bureaucrat and back again. Meanwhile team members, long poised for action, passed around eagerly whatever snippets of news they could glean from the overheard conversations.

They also pored over a faxed copy of the two-page feature article entitled 'Mission to Nicaragua' which *The Times* had published that same morning in Britain. True to his word, the editor had given the project a most positive write-up, and such commercial supporters as we had found had rallied to Brenda Muckley's call. Griffon Hovercraft and Nicaragua's Ministry of Tourism had bought half a page of colour between them, and another half-page was full of smaller adverts from other well-wishers. So a full page was available for editorials. Two of the articles submitted by our former BBC man, Harold Briley, appeared verbatim; so did comprehensive profiles of both Mike Cole and the STEP programme. One of *The Times*'s staff journalists commended unequivocally the work of the project, and reported in addition Mike's lament that the British Government had failed to assist him materially. 'All we were asking is that our Government match the sum that our young people have been able to raise. Is £175,000 too much to hope for? The Government has offered "moral support", but in a capital-heavy project like this, some money would have been welcome.' 'Let's hope that bit gets passed around Whitehall,' added Nick.

One prominent Christian in the UK summed up the wider significance of the *Times* feature when he wrote several days later: 'I don't know how much work you put into it, how you arranged it or how much it cost you. But it was worthwhile. It showed that Christians have whole-person solutions and can be demonstrably capable. It showed mission can be taken seriously and not just in its purely religious dimension. I lifted my own head a little higher this week.' A church bulletin in Northampton read: 'There it was; what you thought you'd never see. Two whole pages in the top newspaper devoted to an evangelical missionary society and not a cynical word in sight. Analysis? It's bold, imaginative, Christian, creative, sharing, long-term, effective, caring.'

Sarah took up the phone cudgel once more after lunch, with Mike hovering behind her. The phone service in Managua was exasperating throughout the year. While international lines were crystal-clear, presumably via satellite, internal land lines remained impossibly difficult. On one occasion, when 'difficult' became 'impossible', we were advised to ring the repair line, only to discover that the repair line was out of order too! Sympathies were in order as Sarah continued to shout her way through these sensitive conversations. By mid-afternoon patience was exhausted. A physical presence was obviously necessary so Mike and Sarah moved to the Ministry of Transport, and started pushing to see Minister Vijil, who had overall responsibility for co-ordinating the project on the Government's behalf. He was out, and it was 5 p.m. before he strolled, smiling and relaxed, into the outer office where Mike and Sarah were waiting, and said: 'Are you having problems? No problem!' He then put through a call to Corinto with the necessary authorisation.

'At Corinto we thought that would be it,' explained Michael Pinkess afterwards, 'but the customs officials broke for a late-afternoon break, so it was after that that they started laboriously typing out release documents. Did we have proof of the Land Rover's engine number? Only when the container was opened to reveal that half the contents would have to be unpacked to get under the bonnet did they relent. It was 9 p.m. when we waved the lorries off the docks.'

The following day's bad joke was: 'How can a container be both in and out of customs at the same time?' Answer: 'When it moves out of the government customs and into the private customs.' We had imagined that the trucks would pause overnight at the agent's then move to the Shell depot, where we were to unload in the morning. But the volunteers dropped off at Shell for this purpose waited, waited and waited some more. When they phoned base they learned of the duplicated set of customs formalities.

Harold Briley, with long experience in Latin America,

The jungle canopy filtered the tropical sun on this narrow
section of the lower San Juan river.

The unspoilt jungle.

Machuca, Diamante, Balas and El Castillo: tackling the major rapids on the San Juan river.

The President keeps her word.

Anticipation on the castle ramparts.

Gasps of astonishment as Griffon climbed the Great Rapid.

A bank-note depicting a British defeat
– an unfading piece of folklore.

'The English are back.' In 1780, Nelson came destructively to
wage war; in 1995, we came constructively in peace.

President Chamorro smiles confidently from the cockpit.

Going forward together.

Expedición Británico - Nicaragüense .
"HOVERCRAFT"

PRIMER DIA DECIRCULACION 27 DE MAYO DE 1995

27 May 1995. The President and, on her right,
H.E. John Culver, the British Ambassador, sign
commemorative first-day covers.

enlightened us. Multiple regulations provide secure employment for rank upon rank of bureaucrats, and the private sector has muscled in on a lucrative industry. Customs agents offer their services to negotiate through the labyrinthine process, and in some countries travellers are obliged by law to use an official agent and pay him a fee. Dennis wanted everybody to understand about delays. 'Though your Spanish–English dictionary may appear to say so,' he explained, 'when officials say *mañana* they never mean "tomorrow". They simply mean "not today"!' When Harold started recalling that the BBC tried for seven long years to get some cameras out of customs in Rio, the team wanted to hear no more!

Minister Vijil had no jurisdiction over the private customs agency now holding the containers. So Mike decided to deploy his two most powerful negotiating weapons, an authoritative personal presence and his almost total lack of Spanish. As the process threatened to stall, he stood in the middle of the office with arms folded assertively across his substantial frame, ignoring repeated invitations to take a seat. Although interpretation was readily available he managed to evade all efforts to put him off with a deft 'I no comprendo Spanish'. Hours passed in negotiation as the agents gradually modified their original stance of releasing nothing to releasing the container with the Griffon but not the other. Eventually came Mike's ultimatum: 'We must finish this process within an hour or I shall be obliged to report to the President's office that the official occasion with doña Violeta at El Castillo is cancelled!'

There was need for some face-saving. Reading between the cultural lines Mike agreed to the compromise of leaving the Land Rover impounded, in exchange for the immediate release of the rest. But this meant that he and Matthew had to unpack and repack half a container themselves in order to ease the vehicle out.

Having waited all the morning, the sight of the first truck coming towards the volunteers at Shell must have seemed a dream. But the doors were soon flung open and they released their pent-up energies in unloading the vast variety of stuff:

mattresses, bags of clothes for the needy, crate after crate of paracetamol, beds, benches, pots, pans, tinned provisions. The team worked fast under a blazing sun. While the medicines went into store at Shell, the rest had to be ferried across the city time and again, on the back of an open truck. Someone rode shotgun at the back to prevent things falling off – or being lifted off at traffic lights!

There were now only four full days before the celebrations in Bluefields marking the start of the great journey. The River Rover 501 would not be able to join the Griffon on the attempt to cross the country. There would be neither sufficient time nor adequate workshop facilities at El Rama to complete the major modification required. So she had to be offloaded at Managua. A supporter was found who generously opened up his engineering workshop where the River Rover team could work away undisturbed. If fitting the 'Dumbo ears', as Mike called it, went exceptionally well, he agreed that the River Rover could be trailered down to San Carlos to meet the Griffon as she emerged from the river on to Lake Nicaragua in ten days' time. Engineer Steve Moody was optimistic about what he termed more technically 'the polygonisation of the duct boxes'.

The empty container was reloaded with over thirty fifty-gallon drums of Shell diesel, various bits of engineering equipment, some food and the large rear duct of the Griffon. As the truck drivers choked their engines into life, the dusk was blending the Hapag-Lloyd colours into the orange-mauves of a smoky sunset over the hills. But Gareth was biting his lip: 'Given a clear run we'll have just two full days to put the craft together before Friday afternoon when John Gifford arrives to drive it down to Bluefields. It's going to be tight!'

Pedro Chamorro of *La Prensa* was amazed to hear the equipment was out of customs. An Italian entrepreneur who had recently imported two second-hand hydrofoils from Belorussia – to begin a transport service across Lake Nicaragua – had waited three weeks for his stuff, which most people considered 'par for the course'. Mike was pleased too. 'I think it's fair to say the Lord has honoured our battling,' he said.

Frustrating Delay

The following morning he was even more pleased. At 5 o'clock he snapped on the light above his fellows asleep on the floor, and announced: 'Gentlemen, I think it's right to wake you with the news that a fax from London brings us the offer of a £100,000 loan.' It was from the secretary of a trust fund who had only recently come to hear of the project's need, and had immediately placed it before his trustees. The loan could be for one year and free of interest, if we were still interested.

'The timing's significant,' said Mike as he squeezed the teabag for his early-morning drink. 'What to say to John Gifford when he arrives tonight had been preying on my mind. Once the pleasantries are over, he's bound to ask how the fundraising is going, and I would have been scraping the barrel for anything positive to report. The best I could have done would have been to arrange for him to visit the Minister of Transport so that after we prove what the Griffon can do on the San Juan, he would have a chance of selling them one. Our craft would then be a 'loss-leader' for future Nicaraguan business. But now I'll be able to pledge a substantial contribution towards the outstanding balance. God calls, man responds, God provides – in that order,' concluded Mike. 'It's God's way and I can't argue with it.' 'And the threat of having to send the Griffon back to the UK after the journey is presumably lifted too,' added Nick. 'I wonder if one of the trustees saw *The Times*'s article and then chased up his secretary to contact us?' But Mike was no longer listening. He had gone off to phone the wonderful news to Graham Gifford, the Griffon sales manager in Southampton. It was Graham's wife Geraldine who answered the phone. She was not at all taken aback: 'Of course, Mike, what did you expect? The Lord does provide.'

Chapter 7

Near Disaster

It was noon on Friday, 19 May. The engineers had followed the container to El Rama; all was set for the first static test of the Griffon's fans. As Gareth Smith sat at the controls waiting for the engineers to stand clear, he reflected on the success of the previous two days' activities. The team had worked well. Intense heat had burnt their shoulders from above and baked the soles of their feet from the metal floor below. At night they camped, without running water and plagued by biting insects, under the shelter of a local church. The Land Rover had finally been prised out of customs in Managua, though regrettably only for a thirty-day period. It now brought across groups of team members to reinforce those assembling the craft.

The working facilities had been far from ideal. There had only been one crane available, which was now parked on a large iron pontoon, the port's main loading facility, just off the river bank. Its lifting gears were in working order, but unfortunately those that enabled it to be moved from place to place had failed, so once it had lifted the Griffon out of the container, there was no option but for it to remain where it was until the Griffon could later be moved away under her own power. But they had got the job done, unloading and refitting the side-decking and the rear fan assembly. Two portable generators, gifted in the UK by Redbreast Engineering, had proved invaluable for running power tools on the pontoon far from a mains source.

Now was the moment of truth. Gareth was given the all clear, turned the ignition key and gently engaged the throttle.

The skirt filled firmly with air and lifted the cabin off the ground. The engine and fans gave a steady roar. Excellent! Gareth switched off and leapt out of the cabin. 'Great! Now let's have some lunch. I'm starving!' Straight after eating, Gareth was keen to begin again. As the diesel growled comfortably into motion Peter Dixon, who was watching at the rear, out of the corner of his eye saw something moving. He turned, realised that one of the straps hanging from the overhead crane still beside the craft was being sucked towards the lift fan, and shouted a warning. He made an instinctive grab for it, but at 1500 revs the powerful fan had already taken hold, and the harness was ripped out of his grasp. A terrific bang was followed by a horrifying grating sound.

Gareth cut the engine instantly. Engine noise had drowned Peter's shout. The whole thing had happened in a split second. Now, in shocked silence, the team approached the fan cavity, pangs of dread gripping their stomachs. Gareth was the first to speak: 'We've blown it. The blades must be wrecked.' He was right. The main damage had been done by a fire-extinguisher pipe dragged into the fan from an adjacent panel. Several of the strong metal blades had been snapped or twisted, and several holes had been gouged out of the aluminium cowling. John Green examined the five-foot gash: 'Split it open like a can opener!' was his assessment. 'It's only three blades. We could weld it,' said Neil Townsend comfortingly. 'The rest looks nasty, but it's just cosmetic.' The remark showed more compassion and courage than conviction. 'I wish it were that simple, Neil,' replied a distraught Gareth. 'Even if we could repair the blades it would be impossible to re-balance the fan. Then there's the secondary damage we haven't yet found. The shock may have twisted the drive shaft. The engine itself might be . . .' His voiced trailed off in despair as he choked back rising emotions and walked away. 'I nearly caught it,' winced Peter in pain as he wrapped a cloth around a bleeding finger. Jenny Smith went to help. The strap had torn away part of his nail.

Gareth was clearly blaming himself for the accident. He remembered having unclipped the lifting straps and left them dangling. Then, in his enthusiasm, he had failed to check for 'loose foreign objects on deck' before starting up. Had he wrecked, in a single moment, an expedition which had taken several years to plan? Peter gathered the team around to pray. With one hand Gareth covered his face, with the other he held the hand of his equally distressed wife, Jenny.

'The good thing is,' said Alan Blake, 'the man we most need just now is on his way to us.' John Gifford, about to arrive at El Rama, was the man who knew more about the technical side of hovercraft than anybody else in the world. The manufacturer of the Griffon had flown in from Britain the night before and taken the morning flight to Bluefields. Even as Alan spoke, he and Mike were heading up the Rio Escondido in a motorised launch. The project leader's caution in persuading John to go out and take charge of the half-paid-for hovercraft during its early operations was about to prove a providential foresight. No one could more accurately assess the damage or determine what was, and what was not, possible. Everyone waited nervously.

As he caught the landing rope and hauled the launch alongside the jetty Mike knew instantly, from Gareth's dejected expression, that something was wrong. A few minutes later John was surveying the damaged craft; he said nothing for a long time. His stony face spoke volumes, as did the way he hurled away the offending strap. For an anxious team these were bleak moments. Mike was the only one who dared to break the silence. 'Can we still get lift, John?' he asked gently. John gave his precise answer in a low monotone: 'If we were to grind out the blades opposite in the same way that the ones on this side are damaged, we might get a balanced thrust – but it would be greatly reduced. The snag is that the intake has to be 100 per cent watertight.'

Thinking the worst tension had been broken, Harold stepped forward with his microphone boom to catch further initial reactions. Our cameraman, Jonathan Allan, had been filming steadily in the background, but now moved in for a sharper angle. While John angrily waved them away, Mike was more sympathetic to the video crew's need to catch these dramatic events. He had appointed Jonathan after thinking of *Amazon Task Force,* a video shot on the Peru expedition by a team member who was a naval photographer; Channel 4 had judged it good enough to screen. TV companies had sent professionals to cover all the other expeditions, but remembering how pleased he was with the earlier effort Mike decided that what had been done then would be done again in Nicaragua.

Jonathan Allan had poured energy and initiative into a wide range of tasks when on the Papua New Guinea project, and had proved proficient with both still and video cameras. Back in the UK he had switched away from a career with British Telecom to complete a Master's degree in video production at Bournemouth University. Mike had talked to production companies but was fed up with waiting for them to get on board. He reminded himself that STEP's central vision is to provide opportunities for young people, so he offered Jonathan a major project which could potentially launch him into a professional media career. Furthermore Harold Briley had graciously agreed to work as Jon's assistant, which would bring a wealth of experience and a vital cutting edge to the filmed interviews. Unfortunately it did mean meeting the upfront costs of hiring a broadcast-quality Betacam SP camera.

Mike turned from the crippled hovercraft and faced the camera. 'What a shame! What a shame! We were all ready to go, but we did it in a rush and we've paid the penalty. We've let our enthusiasm run away with us a bit.' This was not a euphemistic 'collective responsibility' simply covering one individual's chagrin. Gareth probably felt like the footballer who has missed the crucial spot kick in a penalty shoot-out. But in such a case the real problem lies in the drawn game beforehand, for which the whole team is responsible. It was so in this case. The lack of funds in the early months had compressed the timescales so that unexpected delays put everybody under pressure and left no margin for error. Mike was philosophical, but determined. 'We've taken one step back; now we're going to think through very rationally what to do next.'

John Gifford was still struggling to come to terms with the tragedy. 'We've built some sixty hovercraft to this design and a lift fan has never gone before. That's partly why we haven't considered a guard necessary.' But, once expressed, he put these thoughts behind him and started thinking ahead. 'Hovercraft operate in remote locations so they are designed to be easily repairable in the field. But in this case I'm not happy about attempting a temporary repair. It's so dangerous to muck about with a fan. It would probably take as long to do a temporary repair as to send out another fan anyway, but I don't know if we have one in stock; it's not something we would normally have on the shelf.' 'Couldn't one of the supporters who are coming out bring the replacement parts?' asked Neil Townsend. 'When do they arrive?' 'Thursday night in Managua,' replied Mike. As he had promised, a dozen close supporters were coming out from Britain to see some of the hovercraft action, especially on the San Juan, and to be part of the first tourist group from the UK to visit Nicaragua since the civil war. Rather than just talk about the potential of hovercraft for attracting ecotourists to a jungle river, Mike was staging a pilot tour to coincide with President Chamorro's visit to the team at El Castillo.

'We'll need the spare parts way before that if we are going to be there for the President on the Saturday,' interjected Peter. But Mike had fastened on a half-thought which he struggled to mould into shape. 'Let's imagine one of these supporters could bring their flight forward to bring the stuff out. If John makes a comprehensive list of requirements and returns to Managua, the information could be faxed to Griffon in Southampton in a matter of hours. Jenny, please drive John back to Managua as soon as he's ready to go.' Given a clear objective, a sequence of events that might achieve it were now readily presenting themselves. 'I'll leave myself immediately by boat down to Bluefields to phone Managua from Pastor Ed's house. That way they can get working on the airlines and arrange for some willing supporter to come out early, instead of only learning about it when John and Jenny arrive by road several hours later.'

It was already shaping up into an impressive piece of crisis management, but the buzz of activity as the damaged area was dismantled under John's instruction could not entirely stifle the anxiety in people's minds. The rescue plan rested on such a string of assumptions. Would a supporter be available to come early? Would an airline seat be available to bring them? More chilling still, could we reach the factory over a weekend, and if we could, would they have a fan in stock? If they did, would such an unwieldly item be accepted as passenger's checked baggage? Could we get it through customs at the airport? How long would it take to fit, if we ever got it to El Rama? Mike clamped down on such speculation and encouraged the team to concentrate positively on what could be done. But like everyone else he knew that it was not just the meeting with the President that was at stake. The whole project hung by a slender thread.

At Bluefields it had been a day of relentless but happy activity. Ken Pollard's doubled work force swarmed like a small army of ants to every corner of the school block. The previous night a consignment of doors and windows, made at the Bible institute workshops in Managua, had arrived on the slow cargo boat from El Rama. The moment the main nails had been driven in, painters and varnishers began on the frames. The team worked with one mind to get the building ready for Sunday morning. They were concentrating so hard that bottles of *gaseosa* had to be placed in their hands to force them to drink. It was important; they were sweating copiously.

At a very conservative estimate, unemployment and under-employment in Bluefields is put at 60 per cent; many think 90 per cent. A run-down infrastructure that cripples enterprise is a legacy of both the war and Hurricane Joan. Legitimate jobs are scarce, and poverty has driven increasing numbers of fishermen into assisting the Colombian drug smugglers, pushing cocaine up to the United States through the almost deserted shipping lanes off the Atlantic coast. 'How do law-abiding people survive?' David Coates asked Pastor Ed as they drove down to the waterfront to meet the boat the previous evening. 'We call it *chamba*;[1] a little bit of this, little bit of that.' By the time they arrived on the wharf the expedition's twenty-three drums of diesel and the window frames from El Rama had been unloaded. Eager dockers crowded forward, not so much to claim for the work just completed as to get a slice of the more lucrative job of taking the goods on to their final destination. All round the *muelle* trucks moved, horns blared. Huge baskets of fruit were handled by cursing stevedores, the sweat glistening on their bodies in the port's floodlights. Children darted mischievously among the handcarts and the piles of cargo.

The chaotic scene offered a contrast to the stillness David had enjoyed earlier that day when he walked down to the waterfront to check on the boat's arrival time. Small groups of men had been staring listlessly out to sea, the only sound the fluttering of battered bunting on the overhead electric cables, and the occasional squawk of a seagull. Now it was bedlam; every Bluefielder for himself as each sought to hustle some earnings out of the town's event of the day – the riverboat's arrival. Ed quickly had the window frames loaded but it was too late to do anything about the fuel. He selected an older, weather-beaten man from a willing crowd of volunteers to guard the consignment overnight.

David had arranged for a truck to be there in the morning. With its flat bed six feet off the ground it was hardly an ideal vehicle for the job. How to lift drums weighing over a hundred kilograms to such a height? It was of course *chamba* to the waiting men. A gang of four did the job. Ed Jaentschke arbitrated over payment, and recommended that the asking price be paid, on the grounds that 'in Bluefields you works hard, though maybe not for long, but you has to earn enough to cover the days when there's no work to be had'!

In the early afternoon John Gifford and Mike had been despatched to El Rama for what should have been a pleasing inspection of the re-assembled Griffon, followed by a relaxed 'hover' downriver back to Bluefields next day. After enjoying a lively Friday-evening service at the Verbo church, Nick looked forward to an early night, but suddenly there was a shout from the balcony of Ed's house, and there was Mike standing in the gleam of the veranda light. 'The lift-fan has been damaged. But don't worry, spare parts can be flown from the UK by Sunday night so we can stay on course for El Castillo.' The devastating news had been presented in as matter-of-fact a way as possible. 'Get down to the port to help the exhausted team members coming in, especially Jon and Harold with the heavy camera gear.'

Shaking off all thought of sleep, Nick and David disappeared into the night as Mike got on the phone to begin the sequence of events he had so confidently sketched in. The obvious choice to be asked to come out early was Rob Case-Green's father, Nick. But with British Summer Time seven hours ahead, there was no time to lose if Rob was to contact him. The phone lines were erratic but he finally got through and heard his mother's faint voice. Would his father be able to get the Sunday-morning flight? Could he drop all his business and personal concerns at twenty-four hours' notice to leave three days early? Perhaps Mike's commitment to Rob, that wintry January night at the poorly attended event in Reigate Town Hall, was about to be rewarded.

Mike updated everybody the following morning as the team gathered in the cool of the new school classrooms, the smell of drying paint pervading the air. 'Continental Airlines have confirmed a seat for Nick Case-Green on tomorrow's flight from Gatwick. But the most remarkable answer of all to our prayers has come from Griffon. Quite exceptionally they had an employee in their office on Saturday when news of our emergency arrived and, best of all, although they have never previously kept a spare lift-fan on the shelf, they happened to have one! An unusually stiff clause in a recent Finnish contract insisted on a twenty-four-hour spare-part replacement service, which meant their having to keep spares in stock for every imaginable contingency, and even for those which the company had previously considered unimaginable! So Scandinavian – if not precisely Danish – efficiency,' concluded Mike, 'has saved our bacon!' The team groaned at the awful joke, but took heart at his being able to jest again at what was still a precarious situation.

The airline had agreed to carry the oversized spare parts, which Griffon staff were working hard even over the weekend to get together. 'It could all be here early on Monday,' said Mike hopefully, 'five days ahead of the scheduled meeting with the President.

'I'm convinced that it's right to go ahead tomorrow with the school inauguration here in Bluefields. The hovercraft initiative has grown out of the Steppers' efforts in Nicaragua. Look at this magnificent building. It's the highest-standard building STEP has ever put together and it's well worth celebrating,' he enthused. 'In a way there may be an advantage in the eye-catching hovercraft's not distracting attention from the outstanding achievement of these young people.'

At 4 p.m. everyone downed tools, cleaned up and walked to the town's central *plaza* where the Mayor had laid on a reception in the Town Hall. Stretched across the main street was a large banner in English: THE PEOPLE OF BLUEFIELDS WELCOME THE BRITISH HOVERCRAFT TEAM. Inside, the Mayor, Hennington Omeir – who was also the local dentist – presented Mike with the keys of the town, declaring: 'We welcome you as friends. Bluefields is your home.' An unexpected power cut plunged the hall into darkness as a local historian was giving a lecture on the town's cultural heritage and her centuries-old links with Britain. She battled on by candlelight. After refreshments, with lights restored, a full-size maypole was erected and young people wove a dramatic dance with colourful ribbons. It illustrated perfectly the hybrid culture: Morris dancing with Caribbean verve.

*   *   *   *   *

To cross the rain forest by small plane from Managua to beautiful Bluefields Bay (no blue fields within sight here; the township was apparently named after Blauwveld, a Dutch pirate) is, even today, to leave an atmosphere typically Latin and find yourself immersed in one equally easy-going but strikingly divergent. Not everyone on the team was fully aware of how this cultural divergence had come about. Skin colour moves from white and olive to brown and black, creole English is heard as children play on the streets, sometimes mixed happily with Spanish within the very same sentence. Food, drink, dance and popular music will all appear 'foreign' to a Managuan. A majority of the population will profess the Protestant faith, a situation almost unique on the subcontinent. These are not just the growing mass of new *evangélicos* but Anglicans, Methodists and Moravians whose presence on the coast dates back to the early days of European exploration in the Caribbean.

Some picture of the ethnic mix of the population in 1894 can be gained from a petition cabled to London from Bluefields by the Acting Vice-Consul when martial law in the rest of Nicaragua was threatening the happiness of the coastal people. Of the 184 signatories, sixty-two were English or British subjects, forty-two were Americans, sixty-four Miskitos, eight Germans, four Colombians, one Austrian, one Swede, one Nicaraguan and one Chinese! The inclusion of the 'one Nicaraguan' reveals just how removed from the rest of the Republic Bluefields then considered itself to be, and indeed was!

But by then the time had come for Britain to relinquish her claim to jurisdiction over this distant Caribbean shoreline, and that very year she formally recognised the wisdom of its integration into the rest of the Republic of Nicaragua. A hundred years later Mike was keeping this in mind as he planned the project in 1994. But the Miskitos were not to be so easily abandoned. The Chief sent a petition to Queen Victoria dated 8 March 1894 and signed by hundreds of people: 'We ask humbly and respectfully that Your Majesty take our case . . . and not allow a forcible incorporation. . . . as Nicaragua have in their employ . . . men of the baser sort, who are endeavouring by unfair means to bring about the incorporation. We beg Your Majesty . . . to take back under your protection the Mosquito nation and people, so that we may become a people of Your Majesty's Empire, who shall ever be devoted and obedient to Your Majesty and Your Majesty's Government.'

Even today the 6 per cent of the population who face a

daily struggle for survival on the Mosquito Shore are still likely to treat the remaining 94 per cent of Nicaraguans as 'invading Spaniards'! Until the degree of geographical isolation is significantly lessened, little progress towards resolving an age-old problem seems likely. And that is why Mike was often heard to say: 'Properly understood, this is a communications project.'

*   *   *   *   *

People started arriving at the school site from early the next morning. Large Afro-Caribbean mothers in floral prints moved chairs into the shade and began a long wait. A bus hired to ferry people up from the town disgorged a chattering crowd of schoolchildren, crisp in white shirts and pinafore dresses, then was off, with a grating of gears, to collect another load. The day was again swelteringly hot, but by 11 o'clock there were over three hundred locals waiting expectantly.

The VIPs were late. Nobody minded; time is an elastic commodity in Latin culture. They had been held up by a delegation from Corn Island, off the coast, determined to lobby the Minister of Municipalities, who was visiting. Our principal guest was John Culver, the British Ambassador, who had made an invaluable contribution from his small Projects Fund towards the building materials. He spoke simply and with pride about the impressive contribution made by the British young people. When it came to cutting the ribbon across the doorway, in a deft and appropriate stroke of informality, he handed the scissors to one of the pretty schoolgirls whose classroom it would be. She hesitated shyly, then snipped the tape with delight.

Mike made a characteristic speech, with Dennis interpreting (no simple task, this, with Mike in full and unpredictable flow!): 'I've always wanted the hovercraft to be spelt with a small 'h' in this project of ours,' he said, 'so although I'm sorry you are not seeing the craft today, it's not the most important thing. Our hovercraft is just a means to an end. We want to see this school repeated up and down the Mosquito Coast. We want

94

to fulfil the late Pedro Chamorro's vision for the "naked feet of Nicaragua". We bring a first small pair of shoes.'

Mike then gave Pedro Chamorro Junior an expedition shirt with the hovercraft logo embroidered across the front. The visionary's son immediately disappeared round the back of the building and came back wearing it, a spontaneous gesture that told, even more powerfully than the speech which followed, of his delight that his father's convictions were being pursued. He was obviously moved by being treated personally as a member of the team. 'The hovercraft project is an inspiration,' he said, 'and fixes the eyes of the nation on this region. I am moved too by the heart of these young Britishers, giving of their time to build this school with their very own hands and their very own money.' It was a hint that Pedro Chamorro, though deeply impressed, seemed unable fully to understand, as did many others, the team's selfless commitment.

Radiant among later contributors was Ligia Jaentschke, Ed's wife and the school's head teacher. With smiling eyes she spoke simply but powerfully of her own Christian vision to provide affordable schooling for the poorer children of the town.

The week before, Mike had given the local TV Channel 8 exclusive rights to televise the journey. He had recognised that if the company had to charter a vessel from which to film the Griffon as it went down the coast, it might prove a useful means of transporting surplus team members south. With River Rover out of the operation and the Griffon seating only twenty, more transport would be essential if everyone was to get to El Castillo on time. Carlos Briceño, the TV producer, explained that his brother owned a medium-sized vessel, the *Gloria Elisa*, which fished out of Bluefields, mainly for lobster. It could accommodate up to fifteen in addition to the crew, but her maximum speed would be only seven to eight knots. 'She's evidently a portly matron,' Mike thought to himself, but his idea was to make progress like the turtle and the hare, the hovercraft forging ahead to wait periodically for *Gloria* to catch up. Circling around her from time to time would give ample opportunity for the camera crew to shoot the Griffon cresting the Caribbean waves. That was Plan A. But in view of the accident, Mike agreed with Briceño that the *Gloria* would still leave Monday morning to sail the hundred and twenty miles or so down the coast to Greytown, taking half the team to wait there for the repaired hovercraft to catch up. The cameraman would travel in the hovercraft itself. Privately Mike told Nick that if the Griffon had not reached Greytown by the end of the week they were to 'walk out through Costa Rica' – there being effectively few other ways of getting out!

So at 8 a.m., twelve team members went down to the *muelle* to put to sea. They dumped their rucksacks on the dock and strained their eyes against the morning sun towards a dishevelled line-up of rusty hulls, bobbing together some way off the jetty. They were relieved to see the *Gloria* at the end of the line but there was not much sign of activity on board. Departure time came and went. When David spotted someone on the deck he gesticulated to the crew and they floated across a plastic rowing tub on the end of a line and proceeded to tow him out, crouched unbecomingly in the bottom. The starter motor had broken and there were no spares but 'they were fixing it'! Meanwhile news came through that the Channel 8 man, just before take-off from Managua, had discovered that his video camera was not working. He had phoned through to say he would aim for the afternoon flight.

The advance party reset their sights on an afternoon departure, expecting to see a taxi arriving at any moment from the airstrip. But having waited all day, Milton Briceño, the owner of the *Gloria*, agreed to defer again until six the following morning. As they turned wearily to gather up their kit, the Mayor's *panga* arrived bringing Mike back from El Rama, where he had checked on progress with the damaged craft. He had been there and back in the day, and Pedro Chamorro had gone with him. Mike's pride had tried to deter him from going to the disaster scene but, for a journalist, it was too good a story to miss.

The news compensated in some measure for the advance party's wasted day. Nick Case-Green had left London on time after suffering – not entirely unexpectedly – a certain number of problems with airport security over his highly unusual luggage. In Houston he left nothing to chance and refused to board the Managua flight until he had personally seen his baggage loaded. Watching from a vantage point in the departure lounge above, he stayed until the bulky and quite unmistakable shape of the lift-fan had disappeared into the hold, then rushed down the tunnel to board himself.

At Managua, inevitably, there had been difficulty with the customs officers. Mercifully John Culver had sent an experienced member of his diplomatic staff to help work the needed miracle. With the project's exemption papers in one hand and a copy of a *Prensa* article describing the El Rama accident in the other, she pressed the dire urgency of the case. There seemed no immediate way through and the unbending official disappeared into an inner sanctum, leaving traveller and negotiators abandoned. Nothing daunted, and putting diplomatic niceties to one side, she followed where the public are not normally expected to go – some reports even suggested into the gentlemen's toilet! Somehow a compromise was reached. The spares could go but Nick Case-Green's passport would be held as guarantee. He was not over-comfortable about that but recognised, when being driven into town with the precious cargo behind, that it was a very small price to pay for such a gratifying end to his crucial mission. Even if he had irretrievably lost his passport, the Embassy would doubtless issue him with a replacement!

By 3 a.m. on Monday a sleepless Jenny Smith was driving her Land Rover yet again, with the Case-Greens and the precious parts on board, through the deserted streets of the capital and out into the darkness of a long, exhausting road back to El Rama. They arrived at 9 o'clock. The excited engineers pounced on the packages, then steadied themselves and sobered up when they realised the extent of the task before them. 'They are making steady progress now,' concluded Mike in his report to the waiting party, 'but it's too soon to say how long the repair will take.'

* * * * *

Back in Managua, a frantic weekend of unrelenting effort and comings and goings was over. The seemingly impossible had been achieved; God had answered prayer and 'It's a miracle' was on everybody's lips. In the more relaxed atmosphere that followed, a fascinating theological debate developed, about miracles in general and this one in particular. No one doubted that God is still a miracle-working God; but what of the human factor? News from the Griffon factory in the UK implied, though with the greatest tact and kindness, that if their starting-up procedures had been carefully observed, the accident would never have happened. There was no answer to that. So the debate revolved around whether it was reasonable to expect God to intervene in cases where more care in the first place would have avoided the need for him to bring, as it were, his miraculous powers to bear.

Someone attempted an illustration. 'God certainly could, and might well choose to, heal a man's lung cancer, but I wouldn't expect him to do so if the victim had brought it on himself by a stubborn refusal to give up smoking.' 'Perhaps not, but that's a non-starter,' came the rejoinder. 'Your man was flirting with death. I wouldn't expect God to keep me safe if I stupidly insisted on crossing a Managua street blindfold, but I would hope he might come to my aid if I had inadvertently stepped off the pavement in a moment of mere carelessness.' 'But we need to be careful about this idea of God offering blanket cover for carelessness – no-fault insurance cover!' 'Hang on,' chipped in another. 'If we're here on God's business then there's more to it. He has his own name to think about. If Mike was keen to keep his word because the Brits have something to live up to, presumably God will be equally keen to see us succeed for his own name's sake.'

It may not have been profound theology, but unlike much of the genre it was theology forged in a field situation, not theorised in a marble hall of some distant theological college. And for that reason, if for no other, it was a worthwhile debate. Finally, it was agreed that God was not going to 'make a fool of himself' by agreeing to underwrite all our stupidities. Conversely, where our heart is right with God, he is certainly not going to watch us get bogged down in failure as a result of human error; he knows our weaknesses.

Call it what you will, the weekend had seen quite exceptional developments. The utmost humanly possible had been done, and the speed of modern-day communication had brought success within reach. But the amazing chain of interlocking circumstances which allowed that consignment to get from Southampton to El Rama in such an unbelievably short space of time was, to project members, a miracle. A secular team would have said: 'We were dead lucky.' In Managua they said: 'Sorry, Father, about the mistake; thanks for your forgiveness and for watching over our best efforts to make amends. Thanks too for doing for us the things we couldn't possibly have done for ourselves.'

It was comforting to learn later that the Griffon design team were considering whether a modification might not be introduced to the 2000 DX – a guard over the fan's air intake – so as to prevent a recurrence. So the tragedy might yet be turned to some profit.

* * * * *

Manuel Rodríguez, the skipper of the *Gloria Elisa*, was a casting director's dream for a Caribbean sea-dog. Straggly, sun-bleached locks moved in the sea breeze to crown a tanned face, while tobacco-stained teeth could occasionally be glimpsed beneath a fierce moustache. Obligatory tattoos adorned the taut and wiry limbs. When Milton revealed that his captain was a Cuban exile, a final touch of spice had been added to the dish. He proved more friendly than his appearance, though the advance party never quite lost their first impression that he was capable of knocking a man backwards with the strength and meanness of a Cuban boxer. He turned up on the quay at 7.30 on the Tuesday morning after the team had already been waiting over an hour. The mechanic was still working on the ship's engine and had by then isolated the problem to the solenoid.

Two hours later coughs of black smoke belched from the

Gloria's funnel and she moved across at last to the head of the *muelle* to let the party on board. Milton then announced that, since we had been so much delayed, we might as well wait after all for Martin the cameraman from Channel 8. By the time he arrived at 11.30 the soporific roll of the swell had lulled most of the team into a resigned torpor. Precisely at noon the ship sailed. The absurdity of the unplanned exactitude, after a delay of one and a half days, escaped none of the Europeans' notice. They chugged up the coast – northwards! After exchanging surprised looks with others, Nick found the stocky owner lying on a bunk in the main cabin. 'Excuse me for asking, but why are we going north?' 'Don't worry,' said Milton with a smile, 'only *pangas* can go straight across the bay. We draw at least five feet, so have to use this channel before turning south.' And sure enough the *Gloria* presently swept around and headed across to El Bluff, the neck of land which protects the throat of the bay.

The crew planned to go fishing for lobsters after dropping the party at Greytown, so they stopped at El Bluff to pick up Miskito divers. Miskitos are the most fearless and skilful at the task, the best of them getting down to 190 feet, literally to scrape lobsters off the ocean floor. An average catch of twenty will earn them as much as a hundred dollars a day. Manuel returned with two black men. Apart from a knife, they brought nothing but the faded T-shirts and shorts they stood in, their matted, unkempt dreadlocks contrasting strongly with limbs perfectly toned by years of physical exertion.

At last they were sailing south, to anchor overnight outside Monkey Point, a hamlet half-way down the coast. The trip was not uneventful. Before they had gone far they were chased by a powerful *panga* and boarded by an irate character, obviously infuriated that one of the divers had reneged on a work contract he thought he had made with him. When he had gone, Milton gave Nick his by now familiar 'explain all' smile which somehow suggested a love–hate relationship with the surrounding culture.

At Monkey Point, the engine fired before dawn the next morning, waking team members who had spread their bedrolls on the deck. An hour or two later they were in the open sea, surrounded by large fishing boats, their ballooning nets lifted clear of the water. Nick thought they looked for all the world like 'monstrous Victorian matrons clutching bulky petticoats as they paddled in the sea at Brighton'. But the strange spectacle was real enough. And the crew of the *Gloria* were pulling aboard a giant turtle, which lay on its back all the morning, piteously gasping for breath in the scorching sun. The team asked the crew to put it out of its misery but, since turtle meat is best fresh, they wanted it alive until they got back to port. Manuel did finally concede to dousing it with buckets of water occasionally.

The incessant hammering of the boat's air compressor shattered what might otherwise have been a pleasurable trip south. It served to fill diving tanks, and the team calculated, by counting the tanks and the time it took to fill one, that there would be no relief from the pile-driving noise for hours to come.

But, happily, at 9.30 Manuel slowed the engines and indicated that, according to the chart, they should have been off Greytown. They scanned the shoreline for a gap in the foliage or an alteration to the surf that might have revealed where the San Juan river broke into the sea. Only then did the skipper admit that he had never been that far south before! He was persuaded into the venture only by the prospect of visiting rich fishing grounds rumoured to exist twenty miles offshore. The *Gloria* crawled up and down the coast searching for the *barra*, the treacherous sandbar where tide and river current meet, which Nick had passed when emerging from the river in a *panga* the previous year. He racked his memory for some helpful landmark without success. Eventually, at about 11 o'clock, the anchor was dropped and two small dug-out canoes were sent splashing into the sea. Watchers on deck saw them being tossed through the surf, but finally two tiny figures emerged safely on to the beach and set off in search of the village. For the rest, the bliss of a dip in the sea was soon interrupted by the sound of outboard motors. Two *pangas*, half a mile to the north, were cutting diagonally across the surf and bouncing towards them. Mariano, the Mayor of Greytown, and Aldrick, whom the recce group had met in 1994, greeted them warmly.

The skipper was now impatient to get off to his fishing grounds, so team and kit were landed, to shelter gratefully in the shade of the village schoolroom, swept clean for their use. Pinned on the fuel store by the jetty was a notice in bold colourful letters: 'ALMIRANT MICHAEL COLE, GRAYTOWN GIVE YOU OUR SINCEAR WELLCOME TO YOU AND BRITISH EXPEDITION.' The orthography needed a brush-up but it was clearly in English. Perhaps recalling an earlier British venture when a young captain was in charge who later become an admiral, the Greytown community had promoted Mike, a retired squadron leader, to the same rank!

The advance party had travelled light so it took them no time to set up camp. The pristine equipment was on loan from RAF expedition stores in the UK. The bright colours of the brand-new lightweight dome tents, pitched on the grass sward in front of the school, were in sharp contrast to the drab buildings on the sandy shore, but blended in well with the rich verdancy of the jungle backdrop. Nick was recalling his background reading. Annual rainfall on Nicaragua's Atlantic coast, some three hundred inches; London, by comparison, twenty-three! A traveller at Greytown at the beginning of the century had complained that his tent 'just filtered the rain'. Nick wondered how their state-of-the-art equipment would fare.

The Mayor was already pressing to take them on a visit to the ruins of old Greytown. Only later, when the *panga* brushed to a rest against a freshly constructed jetty on the far side of a peaceful lagoon a quarter of an hour to the south, did they understand why he was so keen to take them there. A year before, the place was so totally overgrown that the recce team was unable to visit. Now a newly painted sign declared that the historic site had been reopened in May 1995 with a grant from the Spanish Government. Eight local men had slashed and cleared the area earlier that month. Standing proudly next to the sign was Hedley Thomas, a middle-aged Afro-Caribbean, appointed official tourist guide for old Greytown. 'They also call me Charlie,' he said, as he waited for them to sign the visitors' book, and then insisted on waiving the entrance fee in celebration of his first group of tourists!

The leaflets Charlie handed out dated the foundation of the first settlement as St John's Day, 24 June 1539, when two Spanish explorers discovered the mouth of the river and named the place San Juan del Norte. It remains the official name to this day, though that it should be called 'St John of the North', when it sits at the most southerly tip of the country, seemed, at the time, to be one of those incongruities so typical of Latin-American life. Especially as there is a 'St John of the South' on the Pacific coast which is actually further north! Dennis found this so intriguing that he was at pains, for a week or two, to discover the reason. But no one seemed to know. It was not until he got back to Britain that he suddenly remembered that the ancient explorers thought of the Atlantic as the 'Northern Sea', and when the Spanish first crossed the isthmus *en route* for El Dorado, they referred to the Pacific as the 'Southern Sea'. So, the two St Johns were simply given the name of their respective oceans. It just happened that the northern one was further south than the southern!

By 1620, such were the possibilities of San Juan as a port for ocean-going traffic that Diego de Mercado wrote to his Spanish monarch describing it as 'spacious and very secure . . . with plenty of water and a good entrance, free of sandbars'.[2] Plainly, that bears no resemblance whatever to the San Juan of today.

When the English took possession of the town in 1848, it was renamed Greytown in honour of Sir Charles Grey, the Governor of Jamaica. It soon saw considerable maritime activity. Significant imports and exports were handled by the merchants of Granada up on Lake Nicaragua at the other end of the San Juan river. Britain's Victorian era was to prove the golden era of Greytown. It had more than 150 two-storey houses, built in the English style, some with marble staircases, many occupied by wealthy merchant families from Granada or Managua. In its heyday the town housed some two thousand people. But once the Panama Canal had been opened it went into inexorable decline until, during the recent civil war, there were no more than four hundred people there. In 1984, it was obliterated by a fierce siege and bombardment from the air, and the survivors went into exile across the border. In recent years they have begun to return to the new settlement across the lagoon.

Appropriately for a party visiting a ghost town, they were shown four distinct cemeteries, American, British, Catholic and Masonic. In sunlight dappled by the tree canopy, and surrounded by the jungle's reverential stillness, the tombstones with decaying English inscriptions might have transported them as if to an English churchyard were it not for the buzz and biting of mosquitoes at elbows, wrists and ankles. It was the most aggressive swarm of insects encountered anywhere throughout the whole journey; mosquitoes, the only vital life-force in a dead town.

One epitaph read: 'Capt Maximilian Tosk, native of Hungary, aged 34, Inspector CV Transit Co, drowned on the San Juan river Oct 17, AD 1863.' CV of course was Cornelius Vanderbilt. Had the unfortunate Maximilian perhaps been responsible for ferrying all those thousands of goldrushers up the river and on across the isthmus ten years before he died? Aldric showed them his own grandfather's grave and said simply: 'He came from Jamaica as a boy when his father was working on the canal.' Charlie led along the concrete walkway that had been the town's main street, cut in places by what had been Sandinista trenches, and pointed to a pile of rusty, twisted metal – his childhood home. Tall reed grass grew profusely through the rubble of the Catholic church; a fallen bell lay forlornly beside the path.

In solemn mood the group returned to the *pangas*. They looped around the derelict dredger that rises fifty feet above the water, a rusting monument to the abortive canal project, then picked up speed to plane across the lagoon and back up the Rio Indio towards the new settlement.

Nick remembered that even there he had seen an abandoned church the year before. A board hanging crookedly in front of a ramshackle building had declared *IGLESIA EVANGELICA*. The pastor had apparently been called away and his flock scattered. It was not in use. The memory added to his mood of sobriety and the general sadness of a Greytown where there is little to be seen; ocean and sand, plenty of fish, an occasional shark or a manatee perhaps, and a wild boar emerging from the jungle edge.

Sitting in the bow feeling the cool wind keen against his face, Nick strained to make out an unusual shape by the pontoon half a mile ahead. It looked too tall for a *panga*. Maybe it was a load of rice on a barge. 'Hey, it's the hovercraft!' shouted several team members simultaneously. The large rear duct was unmistakable. The grey mood was instantly dispelled by this extraordinary sight. They scrambled ashore and deluged Mike with questions as he stood talking to John Gifford. It was 4.30 on the Wednesday. When had they arrived? How had they managed to get here so quickly? When did they finish repairing the craft? How had the Griffon coped with the ocean?

Mike explained with evident satisfaction: 'Peter Dixon and I took a *panga* from Bluefields up to El Rama yesterday afternoon just after your fishing boat left. The soonest we expected to return with the craft was today, but we met the Griffon coming downriver towards us! Repair work had gone exceptionally well, so they had left El Rama at 4 p.m. and after picking us up, reached Bluefields in just one hour and forty-five minutes. We parked overnight on the water's edge at the timberyard, refuelled and gave a display on Bluefields bay this morning. We gave brief rides to the Mayor and other local officials, but aware of Saturday's appointment with the President, I was keen to press on down the coast. We headed south inside the bay.' Mike had invited Ed Jaentschke to join the hovercraft on its journey, and he now chipped in: 'That's right. When I saw where we was heading I say to Mike: "You can't go out this way, man, it's too shallow!"' 'We tackled the sandbar at a narrow opening in the bay with ease,' went on Mike, 'but the Atlantic swell was ahead. We know the Caribbean is notoriously volatile, and we did meet a long swell which caused the Griffon to surf. But the four-foot waves were well within the craft's capability, so we set our course for Monkey Point.

'We resisted the temptation to divert up any of the rivers or visit the local communities,' he went on. 'We'll have to leave that for later in the summer. But we did cover the 120 miles to Greytown in just three and three-quarter hours. Not bad fully loaded with twelve passengers and a mountain of kit.' John Gifford had not been altogether pleased that the load caused the craft to buck hard in the waves at times, but they stuck close to the shore in case of a problem and managed over twenty-five knots all the way. The upshot was that the project was now back on schedule. 'It's a great achievement,' said Mike, a weight having been taken from his shoulders. 'A string of individuals have shown immense commitment to put this project back on course both here and in Britain,' he concluded. 'Now, where are the graphics people? It's time we put our sponsors' stickers on the craft.'

Chapter 8

Nelson's River

The boats were thrust out from the beach into the smooth, swirling currents where the brown water of the San Juan poured into the transparent peacock-blue of the Caribbean. Many . . . looked overloaded and top-heavy . . . In a moment all was chaos: one boat capsized and then another . . . the harbour was suddenly strewn with upturned boats, sinking or floating cargoes and struggling men . . . Less than an hour after they had left the beach they were back upon it, wet, weary and disheartened.[1]

The year was 1780, and a contingent of the British army was making a first – and inauspicious – attempt to cross the bar at the mouth of the river San Juan. They were trying to get where the hovercraft was about to go. Up the river to El Castillo.

* * * * *

John Gifford turned the nose of his craft towards the pounding breakers. The sand showed black beneath the arched backs of the fiercest waves. The previous afternoon, with a heavy load, he had taken no chances and had skirted the most turbulent surf to cross carefully from ocean to lagoon as he headed towards the new Greytown settlement. Now, with a lighter load, he faced the bar head on. The cabin thumped hard into a huge wave and fell sharply as the raging water broke over the screen. The substructure scraped on the estuary floor. Engaging

107

the turbo, John thrust forward amid a roar of fans and clouds of spray; the Griffon shot ahead, the water calmed. He crossed and recrossed the bar several times as though leading a victory dance over waters that had bedevilled sailors for centuries. Then he drew the craft up on to an adjacent beach where a dozen or so team members were waiting. Like a peacock displaying its magnificent tail, the rear duct climbed the bank, flashing its stripes, bold red, green and white. The skirt puffed triumphantly before the air cushion deflated and the blades of the propeller, like feathers being given a final shake before folding back into place, ticked to a standstill. The hull sank gently to the sand. To our modern technology, the bar presented few problems.

*   *   *   *   *

Watching from the beach as the military disaster unfolded before him was a twenty-one-year-old naval captain, Horatio Nelson by name. In command of the *Hinchingbrook*, he had been ordered to transport the troops to Greytown, from where the intention was that they should capture the Spanish fort sixty miles up the San Juan river at El Castillo. He was watching the beginning of an ill-considered and ill-fated expedition. What led the British into such an unmitigated disaster?

Long incensed by Spain's refusal to allow free trade with her New World colonies, the British were further frustrated as they saw Spain's empire spreading into the North American continent. There then surfaced in the mind of a few visionaries the remarkable idea of invading Nicaragua so as to force a way to the Pacific across the isthmus. El Castillo on the river San Juan was seen, according to one British Governor in the Caribbean, as 'the inland Gibraltar of Spanish America, for it commands the only water pass between Lake Nicaragua and the [Atlantic] Ocean, and by our possession of it Spanish America will be severed in two'.[2] In London airy hopes were evidently embraced that Britain might acquire new colonies to the south while still in the very process of losing those she already possessed to the north![3]

Nelson himself was not associated with this highly optimistic vision but, getting word of it, pressed to be allowed to participate. As he watched that day on the Greytown beach, he must have realised that the army was 'all at sea' in more senses than one. The major in command had no clear idea of how to get his men and munitions through the currents and up a totally uncharted river to the other side of the tropical rain forest. Nor was he certain what they were likely to meet when they got to wherever they were going. The San Juan had not been successfully navigated – other than by Spaniards – for 120 years. So Captain Nelson proffered his further help and made available two of the *Hinchingbrooke*'s boats and a number of his crew. Not being one to sit at home when duty called, he proposed to lead the party – even at this early stage in his career England obviously already 'expected'! The confident offer from the navy was gratefully received by a less than confident army.

It was the very end of the dry season, a time of year which, with the water level at its lowest, could not have been worse for such an undertaking. Two centuries later the project planned to hover up the river at the same time of year, precisely to prove that the San Juan at its driest and worst, need present no serious problem. For Nelson's party, not even the drenching tropical rains, which were imminent, would improve their lot, for there would be no time for the river to rise to a more comfortable level.

After the initial tragedy, the adventure began again with Nelson in control and Indian guides looking for routes between the sandbanks. Morale had recovered, but the young Nelson might well have thought of the brutal murder of Cook, another naval captain, while charting unknown coasts in the South Pacific, only a year or two previously. If he did it was certainly no deterrent. 'I want words,' wrote the major in his later report back to base, 'to express the obligations I owe to Captain Nelson. He was ever the first on service, whether by day or night.'[4]

The treacherous bar successfully negotiated, the party pressed forward into the forest. The jungle canopy filtered the tropical sun green on to the sweat-soaked group far below as they struggled to haul their boats and cannon over the almost waterless shoals. In reports written about the expedition much later, the river and the climate were made to bear – and not unreasonably – much of the blame for the tragedy which was to follow. 'The climate here is deadly,' wrote one. 'No constitution could resist it. The jungle did the Spaniards' work.'

After twelve laboured days, there appeared through the river mists, some sixty miles inland, the island of San Bartolomé where the Spaniards had fortified a small outpost. Here Nelson led a charge, lost his shoes in the river mud and, as he later described, in his somewhat inappropriate naval vocabulary, 'boarded the battery' barefoot. They rested for two days after the victory. A few miles ahead lay the much greater test at El Castillo.

* * * * *

This island of San Bartola, as it is known today, was the next objective of the hovercraft. The same twelve members who had survived the voyage of the *Gloria Elisa* were to be in the van again for the first push upriver. Lifting the gull-wing hatches, they pushed the heavier men and equipment to the stern to prevent the bows from digging in and stalling the craft – hovercraft ride best nose up. With Milton Briceño, Martín his cameraman and the crew of three in addition, John knew she was close to her maximum capacity. This would take the edge off her manoevrability, which was not ideal when facing unfamiliar water. To the passengers in the rear the craft seemed to sweep around the first meanders with consummate ease. Those near the front could tell, however, by the firm set of John's bearded jaw, that he was concentrating hard to keep her in perfect balance.

Of those on board only Mike and Nick could fully appreciate the significance of that morning's journey. The level of the river was noticeably lower than it had been the previous year, when they had struggled through with the *pangas*. But now the hovercraft skimmed effortlessly over long crescents of sand that stretched around each bend. Peter Dixon, in the navigator's seat beside John, assiduously indicated fallen tree trunks or newly appearing islands on the large-scale charts obtained from the agricultural research department of a Managua university. 'That makes fifty minutes,' announced Nick excitedly to the party. 'It took us three and a half hours last year to reach here.' They were at the point where the river Colorado forks south-east into Costa Rica.

Here the river widens. The Griffon sped convincingly up three sets of rapids over which the recce launches had laboured so hard, and where Nelson's men, with no more than oar power, must have suffered so badly. There were more exposed rocks now but John skilfully threaded a passage between them. 'Machuca, Diamante and Balas.' Mike was reading the rapids east to west off his chart. 'Does anybody know what the names mean?' Nick obliged: 'Machuca was the explorer who first navigated the river to its mouth, and founded San Juan del Norte. A *diamante* is a diamond, and *balas* are projectiles or bullets.'

Peter was cross-checking the maps with the craft's position as indicated by his GPS[5] which, encouragingly, revealed them to be surprisingly accurate. It also registered the craft's forward speed as twenty-two knots. After a total journey time of three hours and five minutes Refugio Bartola appeared.

A ring of huts around a large open-sided circular shelter with a reed-thatched roof on a high bank above the river, just a few miles short of El Castillo, this was where Nelson had left his shoes in the mud, after their shattering journey of twelve days. By the 1994 recce those twelve days had been reduced to twelve hours with the help of an outboard motor, and now the twelve hours were three! History was in the making. In celebration, they brewed tea under the circular canopy. Mike, John and Peter had to board again without delay in order to get back to San Juan in daylight. The Griffon pirouetted in the middle of river, kicking up huge plumes of spray, before leaving the party to relax and take in the idyllic surroundings. The Jungle Lodge at Bartola was set up as an ecological research base in 1985, by Daniel Querol, a Peruvian biochemist. Tourists are accommodated as paying guests to subsidise his scientific work. When the Managua staff had contacted him by phone to book basic accommodation for the team they had found him a shrewd negotiator!

On the journey back to San Juan, the Griffon, with only three on board, sliced a further half-hour off the journey time. As they moored, a delicious smell of fried fish filled the air. That evening, the balance of the team were treated to what Mike described as 'the fish dinner of my life'. It seemed that each local family had offered the best of the week's catch, and the women brought bowl after bowl of different varieties for the team to sample. This generous hospitality, and the simple gift to each of them of a miniature *panga* carved in balsa wood, expressed the community's feelings far more graphically than the Mayor's few words of gratitude. These forgotten people of Nicaragua had been remembered by a group of British Christians with a strange machine, who had thought them worth the bother of a visit. Pastor Ed 'said a few words' and, in the mood of the moment, gave way to hyperbole as he compared the team to 'the astronauts who had stepped with faith on to the surface of the moon. We did not know, as they had not known, what would be the future of the novel transport they had successfully introduced.' But that night, as the hovercrafters shared that memorable meal with local people they had come to serve, he dared everyone to believe that, with God behind the enterprise, this new 'small step for man' might signal a 'giant leap for mankind' in respect of the people of the Greytown area.

When Daniel Querol and his wife Sandra got back to Bartola from Managua to greet their guests that day, they had travelled all day by road and boat. Arriving exhausted, news of speedier hovercraft travel was particularly welcome. The following morning the softly spoken Peruvian scientist told them of his work in an unusual, almost melodic English: 'Three hundred and twenty species of birds have been recorded in a four-kilometre radius of here,' he announced proudly. 'How does that compare with a similar area in your own country?

112

The President raises the Bible she has just received from
Dennis Smith. 'Your word is a lamp to my feet.'

Shoes for the Naked Feet, an oil painting by Stan Baldock.

At San Pancho, home of the Coronel family,
the 'people of the river'.

Ken Pollard on the shores of Lake Nicaragua.
Ken mobilised Scunthorpe.

With the Mayor of Granada. This old capital
exudes a sense of history.

Sunset over the entrance to Rio Tipitapa.

Background: view from the air of water-weed clogging the mouth of the river Tipitapa.

'We call it *lechuga* - how do you say "lettuce"?'

Desert storm – no rain for twelve weeks.

'The whiteness of their saxon skins was lost as
dust mixed with sweat turned to mud.'

The curbstones trapped the skirt as the Griffon
swept towards Tipitapa.

A public relations triumph for Shell.

Happy chaos – like the Pied Piper of Hamelin.

Arrival on Lake Managua, now linked for
the first time in 200 years.

There are a similar number of "useful" plants and we've selected just twenty-five to study for handicraft, medical use and as essential oils and perfumes.' The alert eyes sparkling above a thick dark beard communicated a deep enthusiasm for his subject. 'Sometimes I'm overwhelmed by the range of species. We're obliged to limit the extent of our efforts.' He went on to outline a shrimp-breeding project. 'We collect samples to observe their growth and we have already discovered just how clear the water needs to be for good shrimp. Destroying the rain forest brings soil erosion and the clouding of the river. Our research aims to develop a sensitive approach to commercial shrimp farming as well as a more effective marketing of the product.'

Daniel was positive about the potential of hovercraft, both in assisting scientific research and in developing tourism. 'Last week it took us two days to collect samples near San Juan. The shrimp need lots of oxygen so rapid transportation is needed to get them back to the tanks. And as for tourism, we are much too far off the beaten track to get the numbers we would like. There are three doctors who try to visit the Sábalos area above El Castillo on foot or horseback; they have no vehicle. It would be great if the hovercraft could go up the Sábalos river. Last year' (Daniel was warming to the width of his subject) 'the prime causes of death in this area were pneumonia, diarrhoea, drowning, snakebite and malnutrition, in descending order.' Recognising the extent of local poverty, it was surprising to find the two incidental hazards of jungle life – snakebite and drowning – overtaking chronic malnutrition. But before the day was over, the reality of these statistics was to be shockingly demonstrated.

* * * * *

It was disease too which brought Nelson's expedition to its inglorious conclusion. As plans were being drawn up on San Bartolomé for the assault on El Castillo, tropical fevers were already incubating among the men, and during the following fortnight they were to wreak havoc. By the time they had arrived opposite the Spanish fort men were already dying and the majority of the party were laid low. The ship's doctor had warned them all of the dangers of gastric 'fluxes', but had brushed off the attention of the myriad mosquitoes as no more than a troublesome inconvenience. With the men in poor condition for a fight, it was decided to lay siege to the fort, though characteristically Nelson was in favour of an immediate assault.

At this crucial juncture he himself fell ill. He had probably drunk from a spring polluted with the poisonous latex of the manchineel tree.[6] And then occurred a coincidence which almost certainly saved his life. A reinforcement party brought news up the river of his appointment to command the *Janus*, and he was ordered back to base. Distraught with rigors, and partly paralysed, he scarcely survived being carried to the coast. He was nursed back to some semblance of health in Jamaica, and then invalided home to England for convalescence, where he survived, as we know, to fight greater battles for king and country.

Meanwhile, had the Spaniards at El Castillo been able to hold out for a few more days, increasing disease among the English would have come to their rescue. As it was, the fort fell to the invaders, who must have eagerly looked for some relief from their suffering. But disillusionment followed; it had been a Pyrrhic victory. For the fort was in a disgusting and filthy state of disrepair. In any case, where were they to go from there, exhausted and still low with all manner of fevers? The plan had envisaged reaching San Carlos, still thirty miles ahead, capturing the cities of Granada on Lake Nicaragua and Leon, and finally forcing a passage to the Pacific so as to divide the Spanish empire in two. Such objectives must have been approved by some unbelievably sanguine mandarin comfortably ensconced in London, far from the fearful realities of the San Juan.

Those now in charge sent a scouting party ahead in an attempt to assess the situation at San Carlos. But bereft of Nelson's verve and courage they promptly judged the Spanish presence there too strong to be challenged and went back to El

Castillo. Would it have made a difference to the outcome had Nelson still been in charge? Almost certainly not, for conditions at El Castillo were catastrophic and must, in the end, have been determinative. The fort was no more than a sordid, soiled and evil-smelling 'hospital' for the sick, most of whom were dying of dysentery, yellow-fever, snakebite, and the then little-known scourges of malaria and dengue. The very few still well enough to report for duty were unable even to bury the dead, so rocky was the soil around the fort. A mortuary was set up beside the sick ward, where bodies were dragged until they could be abandoned to the river below.

When some weeks later it was decided that the operation should be aborted and El Castillo abandoned, not more than ten of the two hundred men Nelson had originally led so determinedly up the river survived to get back to the Atlantic. And of 1800 men who were posted at some time or other to various aspects of the enterprise, 1400 perished. Nelson always loyally refused to criticise the planners, and was throughout his life of the opinion that, had the venture begun a few weeks earlier, it could have met with success. He had taken part in a tragedy, not a defeat. When later his portrait was painted he was not ashamed to have the fort at El Castillo depicted in the background. It still hangs in the Maritime Museum at Greenwich.

* * * * *

John was familiarising himself with the river, and his growing confidence enabled him to register yet another record journey time in the second run up to Bartola on the Friday morning. Mike sent the advance party ahead once again to help with preparations at El Castillo. It was agreed that the hovercraft would not tackle the rapids in front of the castle until the following day. That would be kept as a *pièce de résistance* when the ramparts were packed with people, and the President herself was there to watch. So he wedged the Griffon on to a narrow beach at the foot of the white water and beside a row of simple wooden homes erected over the water on stilts.

Dozens of local boys who had just finished school for the day crowded round the craft.

As the team trudged along the waterfront they thought the ruined fort above them uncommonly like a schoolboy sketch of a motte and bailey. Ahead was the Albergue, an attractive wooden lodge that had recently been built, with a grant from Spain, for the purpose of attracting tourists back to the area. The twenty-five beds had been fully booked for the Ambassador's party and the UK supporters' group. So the volunteers reluctantly reminded themselves that they were on an expedition and not a holiday, and erected tents in the patio and on the grassy sward behind the lodge.

Mike was getting a briefing from Embassy staff on the protocol for the next day's presidential visit, with John and Peter waiting by the hovercraft to take him back to Bartola. Suddenly there were shouts behind and they turned to see bystanders gesticulating. A canoe had overturned in a vortex at the lower end of the rapids and was being swept downstream with three figures clinging to it. John powered up the Griffon and sped after them, Peter on the foredeck with a line. He pulled a teenage boy on board while a powerful *panga* raced to the rescue of his mother and baby brother. As John turned for home the boy scanned the waters in some distress: '*Mi papá! mi papá!*' With a sad heart Peter realised that the father was missing, but there was now no sign of him. Returning to the water's edge they prepared to go back to search thoroughly the stretch downriver.

But a group of local fishermen assured them that it would be futile. They knew what they were talking about, and despite protestations from an anxious team, delivered their nonchalant verdict. The unfortunate man would have been knocked senseless by the rocks, held under by the strength of an irresistible current and swept far downstream. The body would not resurface until the following day. Suddenly, Daniel's 'causes of death' became more than sociological statistics, and the tombstone of Captain Tosk back in Greytown became more than a mere reminder of death in a bygone age. Close witness of a modern-day family tragedy had brought both to life. The

116

fishermen's apparent apathy was born of lives lived where tragedy is commonplace. Life on the San Juan remains as precarious as it has always been, and help is seldom if ever at hand when needed. It was good to have saved a life, even better to be bringing hope to the needy people of the river – a pair of shoes for the naked feet of Nicaragua.

Meanwhile the visiting UK supporters (Kim Bruner was among them too, in representation of the families in Houston, Texas, who had done so much for the project) had arrived in Managua and were flying that day to San Carlos at the head of the river, escorted by staff from project headquarters. They were expected at El Castillo by sundown. Earlier that day they had squeezed into a cramped twelve-seater on the tarmac of Managua airport and taken off towards the south. One of them was Stan Baldock, the retired wing commander who had painted Ted Heath's portrait for fundraising purposes. With a sense of humour sharpened by long years in an RAF mess, he kept up a running commentary on the hour-long flight over Lake Nicaragua, and later amused everyone in the retelling.

'The portly Nicaraguan pilot took us up to 10,000 feet, lit a cigar and with his feet on the instrument panel proceeded to read the newspaper, which completely obscured his view of both instruments and window for the best part of the flight.

'Apparently without a glance outside, or reference to a map, he started to let down. I looked for signs of an airport – without success – but after a fairly steep descent felt the wheels touch, followed by a rumble along a dirt track. With trees 200 yards ahead and brakes full on, a rapid 180° turn brought us to a halt beside three disreputable-looking jeeps which were to be the "taxis" to take us into San Carlos.

'The taxi doors were supported with string – literally; there were no exhaust silencers and only woefully inadequate brakes. Even these were seldom called upon. But gloriously adequate horns were much in use as, having jolted at speed over tracks and fields, we finally hit the town, sending people, pigs, chickens, cats and dogs scurrying in all directions.

'Dusty and hot, we fell out beside a dilapidated jetty where a small *panga* should have been waiting to take us the two hours downriver to E1 Castillo. It was nowhere to be seen, but we were grateful for the respite which allowed a can of Coke.'

Stan would say and the warmest admirers of the place could hardly deny it, that San Carlos is not the most interesting or invigorating of spots to be stuck in! It was to be nearly two hours and three or four Cokes later before they finally got away.

The outboard as originally ordered never showed up, so with twilight threatening, they boarded a reserve craft and left. The progress was swift at first and the party were happy enough to be driving hard into a cooling breeze. But suddenly, fifteen minutes downriver, the launch slowed, turned and headed inexplicably back towards San Carlos. Those who spoke no Spanish were unable to make out what was happening, and the one or two who did were too far away from the boatman to be heard above the roar of the outboard. So the party sat quietly in the none too certain hope that all would soon be revealed. It never was. When the jetty appeared again out of the gathering gloom, the boatman shouted something to a colleague on the river bank and, turning sharply, was off again towards E1 Castillo with his boatful of bemused passengers, darkness that much further advanced and the breeze that much cooler. Stan suggested that he must have omitted to say goodbye; someone else that he'd forgotten to feed the cat! The party had taken a sharp leap up the learning curve of what it means to be a traveller in the hinterland of Latin America.

With darkness gathering fast, a myriad fireflies high in the trees marked out, reassuringly for the faint-hearted, the river banks on either side. But there was neither headlamp nor hint of navigation light on the craft itself, so those who knew that the river between the fairy flarepath ahead was not going to be as readily navigated as the stretch over which they were then speeding found themselves wondering how the tricky bits were going to be negotiated in total darkness.

The party huddled into parkas as they drove through clouds of insects and into occasional splatters of rain. An hour later the unchanged hum of the outboards became a phut-phut-phut as the pace suddenly slackened and they were into the first set of sandbanks and rapids. '*Quién tiene linterna*?' asked the *panguero*. 'Who's got a torch?' The visitors scrabbled helpfully around amidships, and finally produced a couple from their haversacks and holdalls.

The incongruity of the situation amused the uninitiated. Why would not years of experience on the river have taught the locals to bring such a thing with them? Others, from the lofty vantage point of long Latin American experience, were amused in turn by this naivety. The locals had doubtless long since realised that, with batteries the price they were in the San Carlos market, this was the cheaper way! But once the torches were found, initiated and uninitiated alike were asking themselves what could possibly be achieved with so dismal and inadequate a means of illumination? The bulbs and batteries from Boots did no more than shine unhelpfully over each sandbar as into a black hole, and on the rapids produced no more than the faintest of reflected glow from a short radius of white water. But from time to time a friendly instruction shouted from the bank, or a light flashing in return, indicated that the torches were perhaps being put to better use than the ignorance of the passengers was leading them to believe. Be that as it may, after another hour of tortuous progress, the pace quickened again, and soon afterwards the welcoming lights of the E1 Castillo mooring quay hove into sight.

For the first time the whole group was together in the same place. Leaders, staff and volunteers, and a token group of supporters; the Griffon itself was poised. The President was coming tomorrow!

Chapter 9

Promises Fulfilled

The only street in the settlement of El Castillo is a pavement two yards wide, which runs along the river bank, flanked by simple wooden homes. No cars disturb the peace, for the only link with the rest of the country is by river. But every Nicaraguan schoolchild knows something of the place because of the castle which rises on a knoll behind the town. It was built in 1675 to deter incursions by buccaneers – men like Edward Davies and Henry Morgan – who were marauding up the river from the Caribbean.

It was during such an incursion in 1762, eighteen years before Nelson led the more official expedition, that Rafaela Herrera wrote her name indelibly in Nicaragua's history books. A British-led party had reached the El Castillo rapid and was attacking the fort. Her father, the Governor, was laid low with a fever – some versions have him dying a few weeks previously – and the defending Spaniards were on the point of surrender. The nineteen-year-old Rafaela ran to the ramparts and fired the cannon. Historian José Dolores Gámez says that 'Señorita Herrera knew how to handle weapons because she had been given a man's education . . . she was such a good shot that with the third salvo she succeeded in killing the English commander and sinking one of the three invading vessels.'[1] By the next day the attackers had retreated down the river. The story, as unfading a piece of folklore as is the Gunpowder Plot in Britain, is depicted on the back of the five-córdoba banknote currently in use. Dull indeed the

120

schoolchild who fails to recall the legend, though most seem to have accepted apocryphal versions which involve Admiral Nelson and the loss of his eye!

Now the Brits were back, and this time their sense of achievement was high. Despite the long delay in getting the Griffon to Corinto, and the all but impossible situation created by the accident, they had arrived when they said they would arrive. Mike was breathing more freely; fulfilling his promise had been a matter of no small importance in a culture where *palabra de un inglés* (an Englishman's word) implies dependability, and *la hora inglesa* (English time) is the local expression for turning up 'on the dot'.

The morning of Saturday, 27 May, dawned bright, though rain was thought possible. Banners on the water front announced: WELCOME TO THE BRITISH HOVERCRAFT TEAM. Others declared incongruously: LOOK AFTER THE SORES ON YOUR CATTLE, and were evidence of a campaign being run by the country's Ministry of Agriculture and Livestock. From first light the Mayor had had his workers out sweeping the paths. El Castillo had surely never been tidier. RAF and ex-RAF types – there were a number on the team – were reminded of the feverish activities which invariably precede visits from 'top brass'. The spirit of expectancy was high across the local population, especially among the children, whose school uniforms were sparklingly clean. 'How can your children turn out so immaculately when you live in a hovel?' was one question on every British lip. 'And how can the laundering be this effective when done on a muddy river bank with a smooth stone and a scrub board?' No answers were readily available, but the questions invariably surface in the mind of Europeans visiting Latin American shanty towns.

The clatter of helicopters filled the air as army gunships circled above. Locals must have recalled the time when they heard such sounds with fear, just a few years before and in much less happy circumstances. But these were the President's security men, who were soon spreading over the town and castle.

By 9 o'clock the presidential chopper, painted silver, was

121

about to land. Ambassador Culver had explained to us that doña Violeta, who sometimes walks with the help of a stick, finds sitting in a cramped helicopter something of an ordeal. 'It's a mark of her genuine interest in our project,' he said, 'that she has been prepared to travel half-way across the country to be here.' So Mike was not the only one to have kept his word. The President had said a year before that she would be on the ramparts to watch the hovercraft arrive and, at no small inconvenience to herself, she had kept her word. But Violeta Barrios de Chamorro is a woman who has done much more than that for her country.

*   *   *   *   *

She was already a grandmother when her surprise victory over the Sandinista party in the 1990 elections handed her the unenviable task of reuniting a bitterly divided nation; she has worked powerfully throughout her six-year term. In a recently published survey of the hundred most powerful women in the world, *The Times* put Violeta Barrios de Chamorro well within the top third. But it is the sacrifices she has offered rather than the strengths she has garnered that speak most to those whom she honoured with her presence that day in El Castillo.

As the Somoza dictatorship had become increasingly inhuman, her late husband had used the columns of his influential newspaper to support every effort to bring the tyrant down. As a result, Somoza had had them both confined near Bluefields, from where they managed to escape into exile in Costa Rica. 'She had been no more than a mother and a housewife,' explains her son Pedro, 'until, while in exile, she caught my father's vision.' They got back to Nicaragua by the terms of an amnesty, but it was to lead to the tragedy of his assassination in 1978, a murder that lit the blue touchpaper of the revolutionary explosion.

After the downfall of the Somoza dynasty, she took the risk – not least, one imagines, for her husband's sake – of playing a role in the revolutionary junta. But it was her own honour she defended when, a year later, she resigned, judging that she was being betrayed by the power-hungry Sandinistas.

During the even more violent years of civil war which followed, she was vilified by the Sandinistas and forced to bear much ignorant abuse for having 'reneged' on her revolutionary commitment. Her home was constantly under siege, its walls daubed with vicious graffiti, but not once did she resort to abandoning the country to find peace in exile, as tens of thousands of her fellow citizens did during those years of turmoil. She must have found the strain and the pain immeasurably heightened by the fact that her four children were divided about what she had done. Two supported her and two, standing by the Sandinista cause, opposed her. But, as all the best mothers can, she has managed to bring and hold them all together in times of personal family need – and such times there have been. The tensions of divided political ideologies, however, remain to this day.

When in 1990 the revolution had finally faltered and the storm-tossed nation was badly in need of a port in which to shelter, it was to her that they turned. When a divided and warring people began to suspect that the time had come for reconciliation, they rallied to the voice of one who, through her own bitter loss and family pain, knew how badly that reconciliation was needed. She did not walk away.

Perhaps there were some very personal reasons too that caused her to put aside the pressures of government to fly to El Castillo that day. During their early life together, she and don Pedro had spent happy holidays on the lake and had enjoyed the solitude and wild beauty of the San Juan river. They had had a love affair with an area which, as we know, don Pedro thought had been allowed to go 'barefoot' for far too long. She shared his convictions and must have wondered if these hovercraft were to prove the 'miraculous pair of seven-league boots' that her husband had dreamed of.

*   *   *   *   *

The spirit of festivities heightened as hundreds gathered on

the field behind the castle to greet the nation's leader. With
the President came several of her Cabinet ministers, none
readily identifiable as such under their baseball caps and
outfits chosen for a tropical occasion and, understandably
enough, far removed from the grey suits of Westminster. Doña
Violeta, however, was every inch the part. Elegant in off-white,
her grey-haired figure was soon striding purposefully towards
the castle ruins surrounded by a nondescript and vociferous
crowd. She carried a stick but gave little evidence of being
heavily dependent upon it.

The Griffon had been hiding round a bend downriver, and
at a pre-arranged signal from the military, John Gifford, with
Mike and Peter on board as crew, brought her into view and
surged towards the castle. As a crowd of several hundred
cheered the returning British, someone simulated an attack of
18th-century cannon with exploding fireworks which left the
sky streaked with smoke. To gasps of astonishment followed
by warm applause, the hovercraft shot up the great rapid just
where ominous black rocks most clearly broke the surface of the
water. John then stylishly skidded the craft to a halt alongside
the wharf, like a champion skier finishing a giant slalom in a
flurry of snow at the foot of a mountain.

Determined that the role of the volunteers in the expedition
should be fully and publicly acknowledged, Mike took with him
six of the younger members of his party as he climbed the hill
to meet the President at the fortress. She embraced and kissed
each one of them with informality and affectionate warmth.

Rain no longer threatened, indeed the sun was already
oppressive, as the crowd ran together on the site prepared
below the ramparts. Both national anthems were considered an
imperative, though language difficulties precluded everyone's
participation in both! The greater part of the crowd sang lustily
in Spanish:

> Hail to thee Nicaragua, for in thy land
> the roar of cannon is no longer heard,
> nor does the blood of brothers
> longer stain thy glorious flag.

124

The remainder did their best with '. . . send her victorious, long to reign over us . . .' The local mayor welcomed everybody to El Castillo, and the ceremony was under way.

Mike spoke, with interpretation into Spanish, and made the compulsory allusions to the Nelson saga: 'He came destructively in war; we come constructively in peace.' The local public would have had no doubt about that, for by now the news had circulated of the drama on the river the night before, of the team's delight at having saved a boy's life, and of their distress at having failed to save the father. 'He came to divide an empire in two; we come to unite a country divided.' It provoked huge applause. 'This is not just about one journey by hovercraft,' Mike continued. 'We have been inspired by Pedro Chamorro's book *The Naked Feet of Nicaragua* to share his vision of the technology that might one day bridge the isolation so many of you suffer. We have brought a small pair of shoes for Nicaragua's naked feet; our hope is that there may be more pairs to come. Now, Your Excellency, you gave us a book which inspired us. We would very much like you to accept one from us; it has inspired us too.'

Dennis, who had been interpreting for him, was to present the President with a beautiful leather-bound copy of the Scriptures. He knew that Nicaraguans are much more moved by verse than the average Britisher is ever likely to be, and he was aware of the enormous esteem in which, justifiably, they hold Rubén Darío, a Nicaraguan-born poet and one of the greatest in the Spanish-speaking world. Dennis began: 'Your Excellency, we Europeans are far too ignorant of your country, but a few of us, fortunate enough to speak Spanish, have heard something about your great poet.'

Darío had been something of a hedonist, but in his later years had struggled to find the meaning of life. In his *Canciones de Vida y Esperanza* (Songs of Life and Hope) Dennis had been much moved to find the following:

> Brother, you who have the light, give one to me.
> I cannot see. Aimlessly I grope
> through storms and tempests,
> blinded by dreams and mad for harmony.[2]

125

These lines – in Spanish such beautiful poetry but, in any language, of such enormous sadness – were so apposite that he had to quote them. The nation, like its greatest son, had been through storm and tempest, was groping its way out of darkness, desperate for harmony. As he handed over the Bible and prayed God's blessing on the President personally, he quoted a Hebrew verse which, had Darío ever come across it, might have been of some help to him in life's searchings. For the words have brought comfort to a great many people the world over:

'Your Word is a lamp to my feet and a light for my path' (Ps. 119:105).

Dennis was delighted that the President, a devout Catholic, had joined in spontaneously with the last half of the verse, and manifestly enjoyed the reference. 'Doña Violeta,' he continued – a more intimate form of address he permitted himself in the light of the warmth and informality of her welcome – 'we offer you this copy of God's Word in the certain hope that it will be for you a light on your path as you lead this nation into peace and reconciliation.'

Before she replied, the President, with no hint of the embarrassment that might well have afflicted politicians elsewhere, flourished her Bible high to all the surrounding crowd, and declared that her first act on accepting the reins of office five years previously had been to pray that God would mark out for her personally the path she was to take. 'English young people,' she said, before turning to her more formal notes, 'may God bless you!'

Her speech of welcome completed, she produced for signature the bilateral agreement which the hovercraft team had negotiated with her Government, and copies were exchanged. It grants the project the status and privileges of a non-profit-making aid organisation, covers the years 1995–1998, and is renewable. The President had herself instructed her Foreign Minister to put it together. She has often taken the route of ruling by presidential decree, a system with both advantages and disadvantages. It gets things done more quickly where Latin bureaucracy might delay a good proposal for years; on the other hand, though gilt-edged while the President remains in power, such decrees are less likely to survive once the President has gone!

A new postage stamp was issued that day in celebration of the event. Project staff had worked hard with the postal authorities in Managua to design it and to produce a first-day cover which would prove useful in the UK for further fund-raising. The results were pleasing; the hovercraft stamp featured the flags of both nations. The Ambassador was delighted. And the President and Mike exchanged signed copies of the first-day covers as mementos.

The ceremony was over. There had been something for everyone, but for committed Christians some particularly satisfying moments. Dennis was greeted afterwards by a number of people delighted by his unexpected item, and by his quote from their national hero. The fashionable wife of a government minister was warm in her appreciation. And a much humbler member of the local crowd said delightedly: 'I'm an elder of an evangelical congregation here. God bless you for giving our President the Bible!' If evidence was needed of the growth of evangelical churches across Central America, here it was. In one of its most inaccessible spots, an evangelical Gospel has been preached and the Word of God is loved and appreciated.

President Chamorro bravely put her walking stick aside as she stepped on to the decking of the hovercraft for her demonstration run, and waved confidently from the cockpit window. As the Griffon approached the rapids, and boulders appeared to her view in front of the craft, she grasped the windscreen frame and an involuntary '*Cuidado!*' (Watch out!) escaped her lips. But the warning turned into a relieved smile as John took her over the rocks without a hitch and brought the craft to rest on a shingle beach. She had one other duty that day, the opening of a children's playground financed and constructed by her Government on the waterfront of this secluded spot, before she was escorted back to her helicopter and took off for the flight back to Managua.

Had the high-profile hovercraft detracted in any way, as even Mike himself had sometimes feared, from the project's determination to serve the neediest of people? The Latins present that day had no such qualms. For them, demonstrating the hovercraft's prowess, far from being a distraction, had brought the team's best intentions into sharper focus.

Mike is not given to shows of emotion, but as he stood to watch the President leave, the helicopter downblast blowing his sparse hair awry, he must surely have permitted himself a moment or two of satisfied reflection. The brief hours in E1 Castillo had represented no small triumph for his vision and leadership. He had tamed a river which had blocked eastern Nicaragua's progress for centuries, and had brought the President into a remote area of the country to meet his volunteers and project supporters, watched by the national media network, the entire staff of the British Embassy and by a large and disparate crowd of locals.

For many, there was very special pleasure in the fact that Mike's wife, Jackie, was among the touring supporters. None could possibly have given more to the project than she, or had more justifiable cause to share in his satisfaction. Keeping step with the man you love, when he is always following a God-given vision, cannot be simple. Jackie Cole has mastered the art; her man owes her much.

When the settlement had reverted to its normal sleepier self, the Ambassador and his wife, Margaret, fêted the British crowd with a celebration picnic lunch beneath the canopy on the island of Bartola downriver. The smoked salmon (where had it come from?) proved a sharp, and much appreciated, change from the curried beef and *chilli con carne* from Marks and Spencer!

But the day's excitement was not entirely over. In the late evening the project doctor was called to a boy on the wharf who had fallen from a tree. Ray diagnosed a fractured femur and concussion and applied a makeshift splint. But the nearest orthopaedic help was eight hours' journey away by river and road. Mike took the decision not to jeopardise the remainder of the project by exposing the hovercraft on a trip to San Carlos over unknown rapids in complete darkness. It was not an easy decision. The very presence of the hovercraft had raised expectations, but as the case was not life-threatening he allowed his head to rule the younger members' hearts. Covering the cost of a *panga* to transport the lad and his parents to San Carlos mollified, to some extent, those whose minds had been set on a more heroic response.

But, lest any had illusions to the contrary, the incident had made one thing quite certain. One hovercraft on the San Juan was not going to resolve the river's problems. Realising the project's full potential would demand much more, with new initiatives and hard work being sustained over a prolonged period.

Chapter 10

Colonial Granada

Bad news had been filtering through about the River Rover. The reconstruction of the fan assembly had gone exceptionally well, but not so the performance trials. Increased forward thrust had resulted in reduced lift and she had got stuck ignominiously on the *lechuga* at Tipitapa. Only garbled reports were being received as to what had happened next.

The 501's absence meant that the team still had to be moved in halves, so an advance party continued two hours upriver by *panga* to reach San Pancho, the pleasant riverside ranch of the Coronel family. Perversely, the scattered rain clouds seemed on every occasion to wait until the boatman was crawling through the rock-strewn reaches before dropping their tropical load; three times the party was drenched. Now another cloudburst descended as they moved into the shelter of the Coronels' veranda. And there, swaying in a hammock, was Dick Bell!

'Just me, I'm afraid, chaps. No River Rover. We decided to bring her down by road on a trailer, but the trailer broke under the strain. Couldn't be repaired in time to make the rendezvous with you so the others retreated back to Managua and will try to link up in Granada later in the week.' No other team member had the experience of driving the Griffon that he and Mike had gained in China, and therefore, with John Gifford returning to England, he knew his help was more required for the push across the Lake than in nursing the River Rover. So he had made his own way south.

The roar of the Griffon announced her approach. She had been to San Carlos to drop off some who were flying back to Managua, and was now heading downriver at speed to fetch the remaining volunteers from El Castillo. Strangely enough, the San Juan is wider in its upper reaches than near the sea, and a hovercraft can power up the straights without reducing throttle and glide – as hovercraft do – round the broader bends with confidence. As a result, the *panga* time from El Castillo to San Carlos had been halved. That day the entire team, plus supporters, enjoyed magnificent hospitality from the Coronel family at San Pancho. Ian, the eldest son, and his sister, who had both recently completed degrees in tourism, were developing the family ranch into a comfortable riverside lodge. It might be thought the family's keen interest in the project lay only in the prospect of its ultimately resulting in more tourists coming to the area. But there was a genuineness about the friendship they extended to the team that belied the thought. According to Pedro Chamorro the hospitality of the Coronels at San Pancho has been legendary for generations.

Don Pedro Senior used to make the long journey to visit just to hear grandfather Carlos talk. And when subsequently the oppression of the Somoza era had forced him to leave Managua, he had lived at San Pancho for some time. Carlos, Ian's father, was a Government minister after the revolution, but as the Sandinistas became dominant and civil war developed, he turned against them and joined the Contras on their southern front, which operated out of Costa Rica. With the peace, the Coronels determined to return to the Río San Juan, for Carlos at heart was not politician, soldier or absentee landlord. 'They're people of the river,' said Pedro simply.

The next official reception for the team took place at San Carlos, the town on the lake at the head of the river. The hovercraft ran a shuttle from the ranch to get the team into place for the Monday-morning ceremony. The poor impression of the place first gained by the supporter group on their way through was readily confirmed. And it cannot have been entirely due to foreign prudishness, for the *Prensa* itself, in publishing its blow-by-blow reports of the hovercraft's progress, had said: 'This departmental capital is an extremely dirty and dishevelled town that seems to live frozen in time.' It was obvious that if hovercraft were ever to be the means of attracting international tourists to the area, which is the Ministry's declared hope, there is much more to be done.

And yet there is at least one poet, José Coronel Urtecho (as it happens, a relation of the Coronels), who has found something to enthuse about as he reaches for a poetic brush with which to paint a picture of San Carlos. Dennis had drawn the group's attention to the verse as the party had waited on the quayside on Friday. It was his own English translation, but it caught the flavour of the place:

> In the corner of lake and river
> houses climb on stilts
> like goats across the hills;
> street bulbs like lizards' eggs,
> air pungent with tobacco, salted fish.
> San Carlos . . .
> in every door a raucous phonograph,
> a slovenly girl,
> a pig.

Such was their long wait that he had wondered if they were to see those 'lizards' eggs'.

However, on Monday there was enthusiasm; hundreds turned out for the celebration. Everyone had come to expect by now the freshly ironed school uniforms, but the keynote of the Lady Mayor's speech was a pleasant surprise. 'These Christians,' she said, 'really care about the poor.' She challenged her listless townspeople to be inspired by the motivation of their visitors, and to renew their own struggle against the deprivation that was crushing their spirit.

After taking local dignitaries and several groups of school children for a ride to the mouth of the San Juan, the Griffon was refuelled with the diesel that Shell had laid down, and half the team boarded at noon for the first encounter with Lake Nicaragua. Colcibolca, the lake's name before the Spaniards arrived, is some three thousand square miles in extension, the largest expanse of fresh water in Central America and among the largest in the world; large enough, in fact, to generate its own tides and its own weather systems off the surrounding volcanoes. Here is the only place in the world where freshwater sharks are to be found.

The easterly waves were stiff but the craft turned north and kept within the shelter of the eastern shoreline. They passed the archipelago of Solentiname,[1] which the supporter group was visiting that very day. These island reserves are among Nicaragua's undoubted tourist attractions.

It was there, in 1966, that a Catholic priest named Ernesto Cardenal began a small Christian commune where his poetry and the paintings and carvings of the peasants has since developed into a distinctive and widely appreciated art style; the craftwork has been sold all over the New World and in Europe. Probably stimulated by the emerging 'Theology of Liberation', Cardenal gathered the small community to read the Bible and dialogue together about the Faith, in the style of the 'Grass Root Communities'[2] which were appearing widely elsewhere in Latin America. Their discussions on social justice, according to him, 'became a Gospel which radicalised us politically'. It was also a Gospel which threatened Somoza, and in 1977 his National Guard swept across the beautiful islands, killing and pillaging. Dozens of youngsters from Solentiname were finally gunned down in nearby San Carlos. So understandably the islands played their part in ridding the country of the tyrannical regime. And when the revolution succeeded and the Sandinistas came to power, Father Ernesto Cardenal was appointed Minister of Culture.

A flock of flamingos, like a delicate pink scarf fluttering in a breeze, rose from the water as the hovercraft approached, and another V-formation of migrating geese swooped to race alongside before tiring and falling back. Soon the outline of the twin volcanoes that form Ometepe island could be made out on the port horizon. In the afternoon they began looking for somewhere to land, for by 3 o'clock at the latest the Griffon would have to turn back to reach San Pancho before dark.

The advance party were to camp overnight beside the lake, while the rest of the team were to be fetched forward to the campsite the following morning. At the first bay the shore was too marshy, but finally, as Peter Dixon at the controls was beginning to look anxiously at his watch, they rounded a small headland and spotted a gently shelving sandy beach.

'This is perfect,' chuckled Michael Pinkess, floating on his back and enjoying the cool water over limbs now free from the confines of the cabin. The team's insurance broker might have been in the pool of a yacht club in Singapore. As the drone of the Griffon's fans faded away, an idyllic calm settled on the beach. With dusk approaching they put their camp stoves to the test but found them working only erratically, sand having blocked the fuel jets. It was an ideal excuse for lighting a crackling fire from driftwood. They cooked up their curry, no less, and watched a glorious marbled sunset behind the silhouetted range of volcanoes, then relaxed and chatted until the embers died, darkness fell, and all that could be heard were soft voices blending with the wash of the waves.

The day had been considerably less romantic for the party trying to get back to Managua. Waiting on the San Carlos airstrip for their plane to arrive, they sheltered from the fierce sun under an ageing tin roof probably designed originally to keep a fuel store cool. Nothing was provided to keep the passengers cool! The longer they waited the more their numbers grew, and the intriguing question arose: how many could one small plane accommodate? No company representative was around to clarify the issue. When finally the twelve-seater arrived, fourteen passengers each had a valid ticket! After five minutes of febrile movement – not at all unlike a rugby team in a free maul with the opposing eight – all fourteen boarded the plane, having pushed their luggage through the windows in an attempt to lay prior claim to a seat. One of the last to board perched disconsolately on the pilot's seat, for all the world like an unwilling loser in a children's game of musical chairs, and waited for the still absent authority to establish his right to travel. He turned out to be the Costa Rican Ambassador who, though not best amused, was obviously confiding in his diplomatic status. There followed a prolonged stand-off between passengers and pilot. The Ambassador was first to win his case and was settled into an appropriately numbered seat. There remained thirteen passengers in eleven seats, and fourteen sets of luggage indiscriminately parked on racks and in the passageway. 'This plane has twelve seats and is not going anywhere with fourteen passengers,' proclaimed a determined pilot as he sat on the grass in the shade of the wing. But fourteen tickets were still being waved at him through the windows, all, as far as one could tell, of equal authenticity.

Somehow, it was finally sorted out and two would-be passengers found themselves outside with their bags, to await a second flight. As the plane taxied, the Costa Rican Ambassador was heard grumbling about 'such incompetence' and the British party watched – for no justifiable reason with a troubled conscience – as the plane sped past the two off-loaded unfortunates, now condemned to suffer further the grim inadequacy of the tin roof. No free air miles for them in compensation!

Sad to say, the continuing inability to organise a system which prevents double-booking is, inexplicably, a hallmark of much Latin American travel. Returned to the capital, the dishevelled party knew just how gigantic indeed was the leap they had taken up that Latin American learning curve in the previous forty-eight hours.

Back on the sandy beach, as the campers awoke to a clear and beautifully cool dawn, they found the waves had softened to the gentlest of lappings. In such conditions the Griffon would make rapid progress to pick them up, and sure enough it was there soon after 7 a.m. Some felt quite 'reluctant to be rescued'. The prevailing wind was already freshening so, with a quick swap-over of crew and passengers, the campers left the disembarking party to pack up the tents, and departed. 'The swimming's great,' they shouted.

Dick set course up the lake once more, and with visibility good he soon saw the opposite coast arching across his bow. 'Let's see what she can do,' he announced, turning the rudder to head out across the lake. The motion was soporific and the passengers dozed until jerked awake by stronger water breaking against the hull. Dick was scurrying the Griffon crab-like across the waves so that she glanced the swell side-on.

Occasionally forward momentum would be bluntly checked by the combined force of larger waves and gustier wind, when the pitch of the propellers would tighten to a shriller note and plumes of spray would be thrown back along the sides of the craft. At such times the Griffon strained boisterously ahead like a bulldog slavering on its leash. 'What's happening, Dick?' shouted one of the team over the din, when first it occurred. 'Don't worry,' came the calm reply, 'we've just been knocked off "hump". I'll turn downwind to pick up the speed we shall need to climb up over our own bow wave again. Watch.' As the pace quickened the spray gradually subsided, the engine settled and she leapt forward once more. 'There she goes. Planing away like a speed boat! Now we can bring her nose round into the wind, but maintain momentum with a bit more throttle to stay "over hump".'

Two hours after leaving the beach, the white cathedral towers and the red-tiled roofs of the old colonial city of Granada came into view. With a final barrage of angry whitecaps, Lake Colcibolca released them into the shelter of the bay and they cruised along the waterfront past the pier and the old customs house. Their combined time around the lake from San Carlos had been just five hours; yet again a promising improvement on the seventeen-hour voyage by the local passenger boat.

The meeting with the Mayor was timed for the following morning but one of the sponsors, confectionery manufacturer Cardenal, had invited the team to stay at his holiday island offshore if they succeeded in reaching Granada early. Dozens of these tiny *isletas*, a short boat ride from the city, are ideal hideaways for the wealthy of Nicaragua. For a Managuan business executive, buying an *isleta* is presumably the equivalent of a London financier getting a Porsche. They stepped onto 'Mr Biscuit's' tree-covered paradise island, just large enough for a spacious villa and a terraced garden. It was perhaps too

136

much to imagine that it might be named 'Bounty' after the chocolate bar, but when Alberto, the caretaker, greeted them with 'Welcome to Tahiti' the idea seemed entirely plausible.

Leaving the party to cool off in the swimming pool, Mike and Dick turned the Griffon straight round to fetch the rest of the team from the far side of the lake. Morning merged idly with afternoon before the 'Tahitians' were prodded awake by the arrival of David Coates and the two young River Rover engineers in a *panga*. They unloaded a welcome consignment of food and personal kit from the capital, but also the much less welcome news of yet another River Rover failure. After just five hours' operation the turbocharger had blown again. The disappointed engineers had decided to cut their losses and join the Griffon themselves for the final sections of the journey. Everyone was saddened by the news; the dream of River Rover 501's participation in the Nicaragua project was over. Veterans of earlier expeditions had perhaps realised it for some time.

Although the 501's problems were understandable in the context of an experimental prototype, they were clearly unacceptable when attempting to demonstrate a technology which, it was being claimed, could resolve the communication problem of south-east Nicaragua. The earlier petrol versions had performed well in the Himalayas, on the Amazon and on the Yangtze, but the new diesel version was clearly not yet ready to face the rigours of the Third World. It had been a high-risk strategy to bring it. Several of the young engineers were to go on wrestling with the craft throughout the summer, and showed great dedication in fitting yet another major fan modification. Meanwhile it had to be admitted that, in the world of hovercraft, the 501 had not yet become what 501s are in the world of Levi jeans! Maybe the frustrations suffered in Nicaragua could yet make a major contribution to the emergence of a highly successful production model. Hoveraid's engineers are certainly creative enough for such an outcome.

They refocused on the positive performance of the larger craft. Pedro Chamorro and his friend arrived in a powerful speed launch to challenge the Griffon to a 'skirmish' on the lake. Jon Allan, trying to film from the launch, was flung from side to side as it struggled to keep up with the Griffon flashing across its bow at forty knots. And then a delighted Pedro became the first Nicaraguan to try the controls of the Griffon.

*   *   *   *   *

With the arrival of Managua staff and supporters, the team was united again, and some turned their attention to the historic city. Granada, for many years capital of the country, sits picturesquely where the massive mountain range which stretches unforgivingly from Chile to Alaska gives way to gentle hills. Behind those hills is the Pacific, scarcely forty miles to the west. Looking east from the esplanade one can well imagine the route across the massive lake and down the San Juan to the Atlantic and, with the Pacific so close behind, there is no difficulty either in understanding why the world's maritime nations have shown, and still show, such interest in an inter-oceanic route through Nicaragua. In the late 16th century Granada was counted among the greatest cities of Nueva España. It served, though far inland, as the country's Atlantic port. Drake's incursions around the Gulf of Mexico and elsewhere had struck such fear into Spanish hearts that goods for the Caribbean and Spain were hauled overland to Granada, and then by lake and river to the ocean. It was this that attracted the pirates further south.

The British had taken Jamaica from the Spaniards, and freebooters were using it as a base to harass the coast. They came up the river to threaten El Castillo and San Carlos, but it was the riches of Granada which really attracted them. Mainly French, English and Dutch, they were drawn together by their common hatred of Spain and all things Spanish in the New World. Their unlikely alliance they baptised with an equally unlikely name: 'The Brotherhood of the Coast'. Pirates who marauded exclusively against the interests of Spain in the New World were known as 'buccaneers'. The Brotherhood had often pillaged cattle from the island of Hispaniola,[3] and copied a local custom of preserving meat by smoking it on a green-stick barbecue which the natives called a *boucan*. Hence they became known, in French, as *les boucaniers*.

Not content with building forts, of which El Castillo was one, the Spaniards took another initiative which, though imaginative, was ultimately to prove disastrous. They decided to put an end to these piratical incursions by pouring shale and boulders on to the rapids of the San Juan river, thus closing the door of entry from the Atlantic. The silting up of the river accelerated, and the rapids became increasingly impassable. In 1662, it is said, a large vessel reached Granada with merchandise from Havana, only to find it impossible to get back across the sandbars. It was condemned to spend the rest of its life imprisoned on Lake Nicaragua. Nicaragua had blocked her eastern link with the outside world, and in doing so had shot herself in the foot! The measure caused more lasting harm to her commerce than it ever caused to her enemies,[4] and the harm continues, for navigating the San Juan remains notoriously difficult today – unless of course you happen to have a hovercraft at your disposal!

Granada still exudes a sense of history which, given so much turmoil and destruction in Nicaragua of late, is not strongly evident elsewhere. The *plaza* is all you would expect to find in a city designed by a Spaniard: the massive cathedral, the tall palms, the shady fountains, the monuments – one elegant marble affair inscribed to the 'Abnegation of Motherhood' – the surrounding homes with attractive balconies and, not least, the horse-drawn taxis queuing for fares.

This is the square where, according to the legend learnt by all Central American schoolchildren, William Walker, having 'burned the city to the ground', threw a dagger into the soil with the memorable one-liner '*Aquí fue Granada*', 'This is where Granada used to be.' Walker was a North American, a sort of land pirate, who had had himself elected President of the Republic in 1855, but was finally deposed by a multinational force which had been raised with not a little help from the British. After leaving the country, he was picked up by a man-of-war and handed over to the Honduran authorities, who later had him executed. There must be something apocryphal about the '*Aquí fue Granada*' legend or there would not be as many ancient walls still standing to support historic plaques which tell about Walker and who lived where and when!

To team members who had seen only the non-city of Managua, Granada held strong appeal. The countryside around is beautiful, the lake restful, the city quaint, and no high-rise buildings spoil the scene. To others the overriding impression was that it is hardly ready for an intake of international tourists. The palms are dust-laden, the cracked fountains waterless, the balconies decrepit, save for a very few maintained by well-heeled owners. Taking a ride in one of the horse-drawn taxis is, the brochures say, 'one of the highlights of a trip to Nicaragua'. Considering the worn-out appearance of both horses and traps, one has to harbour some doubts. The city is marked, admittedly, by a certain derelict charm, a crumbling elegance. Phrases that come to mind are: 'unspoiled, full of character, eminently restorable; ideal for a dedicated owner with a penchant for DIY'. Two men and a wheelbarrow were laboriously laying paving stones across the spacious forecourt of the cathedral, but the rate of progress ought surely to have been concerning somebody somewhere.

A block or two away, a colonial ruin revealed through its shattered walls an interior open to the tropical sun. Plaster lathing, which must once have proudly supported an elaborate stucco façade, was swinging drunkenly down, covered with the must and dust of decades. Locals passed by with indifference, intent on the more important issues of daily living; foreigners, bemused by a ruin surely beyond all redemption, were astonished to learn that it is to be restored. Without denying the importance of preserving the fabric of a nation's heritage it had to be asked: can this be considered a priority when thousands struggle daily to sustain the very fabric of life itself?

Bartolomé de las Casas once lived in Granada. The Roman Church has produced more mystics than social reformers, and Latin American society would have benefited much from more of the latter. Bartolomé de las Casas was all but unique: a monk who championed the cause of the Indians during the colonial period and remonstrated continually with the Spanish throne about the cruel injustices his countrymen were committing. Granada should be proud of any connection with one who gave himself so unstintingly to the exploited and under-privileged of his day. The church and monastery where he lived, like much else in Granada, was being slowly, very slowly, restored. But the guide had to look hard for the plaque commemorating the great man. Finally he found it, dusty and paint-besmirched, behind a stack of timber! Bartolomé de las Casas deserved better.

Granada struggles to recover its past. How is it doing to recover its present? Given the suffering over the past twenty-five years, much of it by no means self-imposed, maybe the developed world has no right to ask. But recovery, it must be said, has some way to go.

The Third World reveals its soul in its local markets. In Granada, the covered area had spilled over into a totally inappropriate street, too narrow for the efficiency of merchants, too steep for the safety of customers. There is usually a primitive order about such places. Fish here, meat there; groceries, bread, pulses and vegetables each in their respective area; clothes, ironmongery, artefacts, plastics. But in this Granada street, fish-heads lay in buckets beneath the children's underwear; liver and lights hung over the pop tapes and the CDs. Vegetables for sale and those manifestly long past their sell-by date sat side by side. A very poor example of the genre!

A generous portion of the drug mountain had been brought from Managua, so the visitors went to a hospital which, until some months before, had been run by the Ministry of Health. It was a memorable experience. The plaster of the rambling old building had crumbled, and was badly in need of a coat of paint. A large surgical lamp once illuminating an operating table was bulbless, rusted beyond repair, and hanging crazily above an empty space; the table had gone. The dental department boasted one antiquated chair. 'We can only do extractions, we have nothing to fill teeth with!' During the visit, the daily power cut was in operation, so doctors sat in poky darkened rooms scarcely able to see the outpatients they were trying to treat. The only drugs available were sparsely scattered along two and a half short shelves – it was the 'pharmaceutical department'. The Managua Government, its Treasury under impossible strain, had the previous year made all state hospitals autonomous overnight – and financially self-supporting. State finance was totally and summarily withdrawn, except for staff salaries (doctors at the time were earning no more than US$300 per month). 'Don't tell our Health Ministry,' joked someone irreverently. 'They'll take it on board as the easiest way of cutting the cost of the NHS!'

A few citizens from better-to-do Granada families, who hosted the visit and warmly welcomed the team's gift of medicines, were voluntarily doing what they could to help the service survive. Brenda Smith, who had seen worse, recognised that the floors were clean, every patient in the medical ward had a separate bed, and each bed had a clean pair of sheets. Something was being accomplished; rural hospitals in Latin America often have less. But this was, after all, Granada, one-time capital city and long a proud jewel in the Spanish crown.

In asking how it was that medical services in a prosperous and cultured city had become so unbelievably basic the visitors were told that the Sandinistas had sacked the place during the years that followed the revolution, tearing out every piece of equipment they thought could be put to 'better' use elsewhere. Granada of course, being Catholic and traditional, would not have been their favourite city!

One North American politician has recently reminded his sceptical fellow citizens that 'revolutions do not occur unless there first exist revolting conditions.' Somoza's regime in Nicaragua was responsible for some of the most revolting political repression on record. Support for the revolution which finally deposed him came from every class of society and from just about every corner of the country. That said, it would be salutary for revolutionary enthusiasts

142

to stand today in the Granada hospital and observe how long it is taking society to recover from their revolutionary excesses. Sadly, youth, so often at the heart of revolution-ary action, never has at its disposal an adequacy of years across which to judge the value or the permanence of its results.

Though surrounded in Nicaragua by human need on a grand scale, no team member was tempted to advocate tearing violently from one in order to supply the want of another. They went to give of themselves, of their own money, time and talents. They had recognised what they had they had been given, and this they were ready to share. Or in the words of Christ himself: 'Freely they had received, freely they were determined to give' (Matt. 10:8). That was revolutionary action too!

On the Granada esplanade below the town stands a larger than life-sized bronze statue of Córdoba, the Spanish *conquis-tador* who founded the colony of Nicaragua. It was a gift from one military dictator to another, General Franco to Somoza, in 1974. The town will not have been as *antisomocista* then, but the hated dictator's name has since been defaced from the inscription plate.

* * * * *

The following morning, Córdoba's head was the only one of a large crowd which did not turn as the Griffon, with Mayor Urbina and other municipal officials on board, skimmed over the sparkling shallows in front of the esplanade. The mood was once again of celebration. The official reception took place in the Town Hall next to the crumbling cathedral in the centre. The drab, sun-bleached exterior hid ornately decorated rooms and mosaic-tiled patios within. In one such colourful patio, the speeches were made in the shade of a cool, frescoed portico where the Mayor received his copy of the by now customary Bible.

While thirsts were being quenched in a leisurely fashion around an enormous supply of drinks provided, Mike was itching to get on with the journey. As soon as a full load had been mustered back on board the Griffon he snapped the hatches shut and launched what he knew would be the make-or-break leg of the cross-isthmus attempt.

Chapter 11

Desert Storm

With the wind in favour the Griffon accelerated across to the north-east corner of the lake in just half an hour. The map indicated the mouth of the Río Tipitapa as a narrow channel running obliquely to the shore. There were no helpful landmarks, and at first the Griffon missed it. Peter spotted a gap in a line of poles which must have been for fishermen's nets, and cornered the craft through on a hunch that it was the way in.

He was right. They were immediately in a neck of water that narrowed threateningly until it was no wider than the craft. Crawling along this 'windpipe' of a river for half an hour they emerged into a rippling lagoon several miles wide, as if into its more spacious 'lungs'. But the river mouth was still in hiding. The map and GPS together indicated where it should be, but they recognised that a shallow expanse of water could not be expected to hold its shape for long in relation to the map. They could see herons standing where they thought it ought to be, indicating a depth of only a few centimetres. Mike hovered into one promising bay only to find that he was heading straight for an unbroken bank. As hovercraft have neither reverse gear nor brakes he was forced to 'dump' the craft; chopping the throttle and blocking the thrust to deflate the skirt he grated safely on to the lagoon bed short of the bank. After investigating several other blind alleys they were forced to ask directions of three men fishing from a dugout canoe. With the Griffon ticking over yards away, Nick jumped into shin-high water and splashed towards them. It was a father and his two sons. They confidently pointed towards a hut and reeds, neither of which Nick could make out, so finally he invited the man to pilot them in. Antonio agreed and boarded the Griffon; he must have felt as if he were being taken captive by strange aliens and forced to board their UFO!

He guided them straight towards a high bank of reeds which, it seemed to Mike, must prove another dead end. Antonio smiled. At the very last moment, the reeds parted and they squeezed through the narrowest of funnels, the fans blowing back the reeds on either side. Mike was concentrating intensely. 'If this gets any narrower . . .' he began. But to his relief, as they spun round a bend, they found themselves in a much wider reach, where marshes gave way to cultivation, trees lined grass-covered banks and, for a moment, Mike was tempted to imagine himself on the Wye in Herefordshire. Minutes later a distant stretch of brilliant green across the river woke him from his reverie: the *lechuga*!

The prevailing wind had blown the weed into a compact mat, fitted like wall-to-wall carpet into every contour of the river. Mike dropped his passengers to walk to the next stop-over point, the Coronels' other ranch at Hato Grande, which was now only a few fields away. Meanwhile the Griffon turned to fetch the other half of the team from Granada and to take Antonio back to his fishing.

As the advance party climbed over the gate on one side of the ranch a fleet of four-wheel-drives appeared and disgorged the entire Coronel clan, or rather most of its males. Carlos had been to Managua to gather his two brothers and their children to welcome the British to the ranch with something like a dozen cousins. 'It will be a remarkable achievement if you make it,' Carlos had said. 'No one has crossed from Lake Nicaragua to Lake Managua through the Tipitapa river since an earthquake altered its bed two hundred years ago. Lake Managua, without an outlet, is stagnant and dead. It collects all the city's garbage too, so it's putrid as well!'

They ran to the bank as the Griffon could be heard approaching, and saw her racing towards the *lechuga* barrier with fans blasting at full power. She shot across the carpet, velocity only slightly checked by her skirt rubbing against the leathery stems of weed. Leaving a bobbing green swathe behind him, Mike swung the craft to rest beneath the ranch house. So far so good. The reunited team splashed themselves in celebration, Grand Prix style, with the hose which was filling the Coronels' swimming pool. Apparently they had had to 'dump' the craft again on the second trip, suddenly and unceremoniously, in yet another blind alley. Jon was filming outside at the time, and as the deck lurched unannounced beneath him he was shot on to the bank. Mindful of the thousands of pounds' worth of equipment on his shoulder, he was relieved to have landed on his feet and to have managed to stay that way as the momentum propelled him up the bank. The kit safe, he was able to join in the laughter the spectacle had caused.

'Clothe yourself with compassion, kindness, humility, gentleness and patience' (Col. 3:12–13) read Mike from the New Testament during team prayers the following morning. 'We are going to need patience with each other today as we get the craft moving forward. Once over the rest of the "lettuce" we shall have to haul her out and along a six-mile stretch of roadway to Tipitapa. We meet the Mayor on the forecourt of the Shell garage at 10 a.m. tomorrow. The Griffon will be much less manoeuvrable over land. We'll only make it if we work as a team,' Mike warned.

An encouraging start was made as Dick wriggled the Griffon free of the mud and reeds into which she had settled overnight, and turned upriver. 'River' was something of a misnomer, for in many places the weeds were so profuse that the flowing water seemed to have been sucked dry. Substantial vegetation had taken root. With the majority of the team walking, Dick had one member on deck each side of the cabin to fend off the bushes. The craft gained momentum briskly and churned around the bend in a haze of shredded foliage and disturbed insects. It was an hour later that the walkers caught up. The Griffon was resting on the bank, her gull-wing hatches open, looking uncommonly like a sunbather lying with hands behind head and elbows in the air.

147

The whole team was now available at the spot where the agile Nicaraguan had performed his human catapult act several weeks earlier. Steve Moody was appointed director of operations, and the team divided into two side-by-side tug-of-war crews, their parallel ropes tied to the Griffon's nose. At Steve's signal Dick opened the throttle and the teams leant back hard. The craft roared forward to the brink of the steep slope, then sank back. At the second attempt more engine thrust and maximum team tug brought her growling up the slope. When the huge clouds of dust had settled she was on the level. It was only 9.30; the positive start was being maintained.

The next task was to get her into a field through a gap between fence posts. As Dick took her in, the stern suddenly slewed dangerously close to the stakes, and it was realised that there would have to be lateral guide ropes as well. It had not rained for days so vortices of dust were sucked up by the powerful fans, cutting the driver's visibility almost to nil. The fan noise obliterated shouted instructions as well, so Steve was obliged to stand on the front of the craft to give the driver visual indications. The cushion filled again, the rope gangs pulled the stern round, and the craft shot into the field. The back-end crew emerged spluttering from the brown clouds and rubbing dirt from stinging eyes.

As this was obviously going to be the continuing pattern, T-shirts were abandoned and every available mask and pair of welding goggles was appropriated from the engineers' equipment box; others improvised whatever protection they could. The Griffon spurted ahead through the next gate, but when the team ran panting to catch up they found that a post had torn a four-inch gash in the rubber skirt. Though the loss of pressure from the air cushion would be negligible, it was a warning that extra caution was essential if damage of a more serious nature was to be avoided.

With a quick burst of the fans, and the usual storm of dust, the craft reached the road. The sight was highly encouraging. The rutted track had been re-graded into a smooth gravel surface, a neat mound of surplus aggregate running along either side like the turnings of a snowplough. The Griffon was quickly lined up in the middle but, although the rudders were perfectly aligned, the craft insisted on careering down to one side after just a few yards and had to be hauled back to the crown. On the next attempt she slipped the other way. The encouragement evaporated as it was realised that the Griffon was trying to fly along a knife-edge. Dick climbed out to discuss the problem with Steve. 'To steer a hovercraft safely,' they explained to the others, 'you have to have a good seal between the air cushion (on which she moves) and the surface underneath, whether road or river. On this convex camber the air's escaping from one side of the skirt or the other, and there's no grip for the rudders to work against.' As Dick wiped the sweat from his neck he added sombrely: 'We can't correct the drift; she's always going to slip down the camber.'

They tried to produce a better seal by utilising the slight hollow at the side of the road, and some improvement resulted, but progress was painfully slow. Dick's other major problem was the dust. After crawling ten to fifteen yards it was so thick he was obliged to cut the engine. Peter Dixon faced the pilot and walked backwards down the road, like a member of ground crew guiding a jet into an airport parking bay. He had no day-glow bats but since both men were former RAF pilots they knew the code for the visual signals well enough. Peter would cross his arms immediately to indicate an emergency stop, and the rope crews would heave the craft straight again for Dick to grope a few more yards through the dust-cloud.

After an hour and a half they had covered two-thirds of a mile. The sun rose higher and members began to suffer heat exhaustion, their rising nausea compounded by dust and fumes. Rope gangs were frequently swapped but by noon everyone was beginning to flag, and a break was called. A bemused local – delighted at least that their coming had prompted the Government to improve the minor road which his community had had to struggle with for years – allowed them to draw water from his well to wash off the worst of the grime.

As they rested, a tanker arrived to sprinkle the road, presumably from the Ministry of Transport or the Mayor of Tipitapa. Unfortunately the thirsty ground and the greedy heat had soon licked the water up. When they renewed the sporadic crawl in the early afternoon, there was little to show for it. But as the road levelled and widened, progress improved. Pedro Chamorro and a cameraman from *La Prensa*, arriving from Managua, were amazed at the spectacle. The next edition carried graphic pictures of an operation they entitled 'Desert Storm'. One heading read: LIKE THE GULF WAR! Wrote Pedro: 'The whiteness of their Saxon skins was lost as dust mixed with sweat and turn to mud. You could only tell they were foreigners by the blue of their eyes and the accents – indisputably British!'

Irrigation channels posed a different threat during the afternoon as the craft inched carefully across concrete bridges with a vertical drop on either side. Had the Griffon fallen, only a crane could have lifted her out.

At 4.30 sights were set on a farm building a quarter of a mile ahead, and it was resolved to park there for the night. Two or three slept in the craft and the rest were ferried back to Hato Grande. The Mayor's assistant showed up to ask anxiously after the estimated time of arrival in Tipitapa next day. Nick was discouraged by the limited progress: 'It couldn't possibly be before midday,' he announced. Inwardly he feared the reception might need to be postponed for twenty-four hours! The town was still four miles away.

At the Coronels' ranch the team looked grimly at the blocked-up camping stoves and the rusty tins of curry. But all murmurings ceased when Matthew and Sarah turned up unexpectedly from the capital with a portion of chicken and chips all round! Mike announced a 3.45 start in the morning! That night they joined in fervent prayer for rain.

It was just before midnight when the storm broke. Some got up to dance in torrents of water, others lay smiling under their mosquito nets as they listened to a thunderous drumming on the roof which was to continue sporadically throughout the early hours. The first rope gang had a double encouragement.

Physically they were boosted by the rain that had laid low the dust; psychologically, by the knowledge that the long threatening road had already thrown at them its worst. The knack of guiding the craft was being mastered and, with increasing confidence and power, they moved up a two-mile gradient and reached the rubbish tip on the outskirts of the town by daylight.

Dozens of children were dotted across the smouldering mounds of refuse, picking it over for something to eat or sell. They wore threadbare T-shirts and plastic sandals. It was no game; silently, and with impassive faces, they raked mechanically across the garbage. The team were shocked by the harrowing sight but could do nothing for the children save share a Pepsi from their ample supply. There was no possibility of letting the Griffon's fans stir up the stinking stuff into their faces. Permission had been given to reach the road from this point by cutting across a cornfield. Having cajoled the craft along foot by foot for twenty-four hours, it was delightful to watch her run into that field like a heifer freed from a dank cowshed running into fresh pasture!

Now, with only the slightest touch on her tethers, the Griffon swept to the town's boundary. Five hundred yards away at the top of a gradual incline, bright red and yellow flags could be seen fluttering their welcome at the Shell filling station. The highway was, happily, a little wider than the craft, and the kerbstones trapped the skirt on either side so that she rolled up the slope as though on rails. A triumphant Mike stood directing Dick on to the forecourt, where the craft slipped to rest squarely between the diesel pumps. It was 9.05. Almost an hour to spare!

There was time for a quick hose-down. The service station had been freshly painted, and Shell's executive staff turned up with three attractive fashion models in outfits designed to bring a touch of glamour to the occasion. There was more than a touch of noise to the local brass band that struck up beneath the bunting. The attendants on that Tipitapa forecourt, bright in their new overalls, had surely never pumped diesel into such a strange tank! It was a public relations triumph for Shell, and a grateful team felt they deserved it.

The real significance of the arrival in Tipitapa was not lost on those members of the business community who heard the Mayor welcome the team. The town's priest was there too, dressed simply in an open-necked shirt. 'Tipitapa,' he said, 'has 120,000 inhabitants, eighty per cent are under the age of seventeen, and seventy per cent of the employable are unemployed.' Clearly a priest of the people, he spoke with passion about the poverty of his flock, but saw the journey as 'a ray of light at the end of a long tunnel' for Tipitapa. So Nicaraguans were beginning to appreciate the importance of opening up communications in the east of the country. 'We've demonstrated that the Tipitapa route could be re-established,' said Mike. 'I have a vision that one day we could see the river here dredged and the lakes reconnected. It would revitalise the town.'

But Lake Managua was still several miles distant, so as soon as he could decently get away, Mike had the bulky craft turned in the narrow street and, with a crowd trailing behind, the Griffon headed again for a grassy field. Heavy trucks could already be seen on the road, the Nicaraguan stretch of the Pan-American highway, which runs east to west parallel to Lake Managua's southern shore.

As the Griffon reached the roadway the Spanish-speakers negotiated with the local police for the closure of what is effectively the country's 'M1'. The necessary permission had been granted weeks before, but now a hassled patrolman dashed between the craft and his superiors. Finally they parked two patrol cars a mile apart, across opposite carriageways; as a juggernaut shuddered to a halt, the Griffon swung out on to the wide road and hovered forward. With traffic impatient to be on the move again it was as well that there was less than a mile to cover before turning right on to a muddy track lined by simple homes.

By now Dick had gained an exceptional feel for the job, and with the Tipitapa locals still in attendance there were many willing hands to correct the drift when required. A carnival atmosphere developed. Children scampered around 'playing aeroplanes' in the blast, the team hard-pressed to keep them safe. The camera crew's pick-up was mobbed by excited boys; too many clambered aboard. The whole thing became total, happy chaos. The throng was continually growing as others tagged along whenever the Griffon, like the Pied Piper of Hamelin, passed an inhabited door!

At last trees and scrubland gave way to reeds and marshes; the ground became spongy underfoot. Locals moved canoes to safety as the craft eased into a narrow reed-infested watercourse a hundred yards short of the lake. Dick opened the throttle and charged at the shimmering water. At 1.30 on the Friday, the Griffon streamed on to Lake Managua; the fans roared and the fingers of the gleaming black skirt danced on the frothing surface. Like a beached whale pushed back to a happy reunion with the ocean, the Griffon swished delightedly away, and the volunteers watched her go with no less satisfaction. Though utterly exhausted after their desert storm, the team knew they had taken part in a remarkable leg of the journey. For the first time for more than two hundred years the lakes had been linked but, more importantly, the disastrous divide between urban Nicaragua and its abandoned south-eastern coast had been bridged. There was more hope for the Mosquito Shore.

Chapter 12

Journey's End

Dr Arnoldo Alemán, the powerful Mayor of Managua, raised his binoculars to his eyes and scanned the surface of the lake. Stretched above him on the promenade was the banner of welcome to which we were becoming accustomed. With the hovercraft nowhere in sight, he joked with his aides about the likelihood of the British showing up with their characteristic punctuality. At five minutes to four o'clock the hundreds gathered on the *malecón* began jostling each other and pointing to a small blur a mile out over the grey water. The sunlight reflected a momentary flash from the Griffon's windscreen and, as she raced nearer over the slight swell, the spectators could soon make out the red lifejacket of a crew member standing on the deck.

At 4.00 p.m. precisely, Mike leapt off the deflating skirt on to a stretch of wasteland, in full view of the crowd on the promenade above. Mike must have enjoyed, as did all his team, a sense of deep satisfaction that after two years of preparation, countless delays, fundraising battles, the near disaster at El Rama and the more recent struggle at Tipitapa, this was the end of an extraordinary journey. We had kept faith with expectations regarding English punctuality and, rather more quaintly, had turned up just in time for tea!

The buzzing crowds parted to let Mike pass. Once more he was keen to project a youthful emphasis even though that meant pushing to the front those with the filthiest T-shirts! It had been the youngest who in general had still had the energy to heave the craft through the later stages of the Tipitapa dust storm.

The plump and cheerful Mayor assured us that our dishevelled state added only a note of authenticity to our claim to be 'explorers'. He presented Mike with a certificate proclaiming him a 'Distinguished Guest' of the city, and Mike responded briefly. 'Our journey of 395 miles by hovercraft across your country has been unique in its linking of ocean, rivers and lakes. It marks for you all a new hope,' he declared confidently. Over a blaring loudspeaker system, an aide gave the general public the Mayor's invitation to be present two days later when he was to board the Griffon.

The crowd milled around and it was again a joy to have the whole project team present, including on this occasion even the Griffon sales manager, Graham Gifford, and his wife, Geraldine. Press and TV cameras were attempting to interview as many people as possible. Tired team members were trying to understand the questions and, at the same time, keep at bay the prying fingers of countless excited children who were surrounding the craft.

Gradually the crowd drifted away, and the week-long programme on Lake Managua had begun. As the craft was parked on the open lake front, a shift rota was needed of pairs of team members responsible for guard duty by night and day. The craft was to be constantly surrounded by children that week, and the team came to develop a robust relationship with them. Twenty or thirty were homeless street children, both boys and girls, who seemed to bed down in the immediate vicinity. They looked about twelve years old but several turned out to be considerably older; malnutrition and sickness had presumably stunted their growth. Their hunger was being appeased by occasional sniffs from glue bags which they hid under tatty T-shirts. Some of the clothes gifted from the UK came in useful. Though they scuffled to grasp each item as we lifted it out, it was noticeable that a pile of garments always finished up at the feet of each gang leader. Later in the day, we found some of them trying to sell things at the traffic lights, and wondered if we should be disturbed at the sight.

The answer depended on what they were likely to buy with the money; would it be bread or would it be glue? Christ once said: 'It is more blessed to give than to receive' (Acts 20:35) which, as every giver knows, is very true. But to receive is easy! Giving – if you want it to be wise and effective – is much more difficult!

A few days later Harold Briley was heard on BBC World Service describing the scene to which he awoke that Sunday morning after having been on hovercraft guard duty the night before. 'As the sun rises over Lake Managua, no place on earth could be more peaceful. I can hear only the birds, and wavelets lapping the lake shore. It is hard to imagine that this is precisely where I discovered so many bodies in the blood-soaked days of revolution, full of images of death, destruction and the noise of battle. It's a new Nicaragua now, dreaming of a better future – a future to which my young British companions are making a distinctive contribution.'

Later that day, the tranquillity was shattered by happy crowds of Managuans determined to enjoy their Sunday afternoon. There seemed to be thousands swarming over the terraces and ornamental fountains that form part of a lake-front recreational area. We were soon to discover that we were not the only, nor the major, attraction. Some had come to see a wildly popular Nicaraguan rock band that was due to perform later. Mayor Alemán had staged a free open-air concert for the city, and we had been cast as the afternoon 'warm-up act'!

The re-landscaping of the *malecón* had been one of the most visible achievements of Mayor Alemán's period in office. It had been made known that he would be running for President in 1996, and these Sunday activities, on his favourite project site, were a popularity bid in his pre-election campaign.

While waiting for the Mayor to arrive it was photo time for the whole group of volunteers. The hovercraft team was joined by Steppers from Bluefields and Nueva Guinea, who had taken a well-deserved break to share in the celebrations at Managua. Fifty-eight in all posed beneath a twenty-five-foot Shell hoarding with a WELCOME in huge red and blue lettering and, as a subtitle, *'Zapatos para los pies descalzos de Nicaragua'*. Even our slowest Spanish learners had picked up 'Shoes for the naked feet' by now.

Don Arnoldo's car was mobbed as soon as it stopped, but his bodyguards pushed a passage through the crowds. People cheered and attempted to slap his back; angry shouts were heard too. The Mayor's smile was confident enough before the back-slappers but rather more tentative when being jostled. Struggling down the steps to the shore he was finally able to greet some of the team, and with a last wave to the citizens massed above he disappeared under the Griffon's hatch. Peter Dixon cruised past the *malecón* several times, putting the craft through its paces like a horse in a display of dressage, before taking the Mayor further out in a canter over the waves.

Pandemonium broke out again as he stepped ashore. We realised that with no area cordoned off, a formal reception would be impossible, and had not perhaps been envisaged. The Mayor, propelled back to the safety of his vehicle by the press of the crowd, had gone. Dennis was left holding the Bible he had been expecting to present, and Mike stood with a pair of children's sports shoes he had been intending to use as a visual aid in his 'shoes for the naked feet' speech! There was only one recourse left open to him. He turned spontaneously to the nearest shoeless street kid and handed them over. The lad had been eyeing them for some time anyway!

The plan was now to operate the craft on Lake Managua for a week in order to demonstrate its potential to as wide a group of the public as possible. Mike briefed the team: 'The cross-country trip has caught the imagination of the Nicaraguan people. We must now grasp the opportunity to consolidate this enthusiasm and turn it into long-term goodwill for the continuing project. We have allocated a full day's operation to each of our major sponsors, partly to say thank you, partly to build relationships for the future. We shall also be welcoming various members of Government and the diplomatic community, as well as local church leaders.'

The fear that the public might think the Hovercraft only related to VIPs was soon imaginatively allayed by the Pepsi company, who placed a full-page advertisement in *La Prensa*. Under cartoons of Spiderman and the Incredible Hulk, and over a picture of the Griffon, they ran the slogan: 'Your super-heroes invite you to take off in this ship.' 'Come this Sunday to the *malecón* with your album full of Pepsi cards. The first 500 children to present their completed "Marvels and Monsters" will take a ride in the British hovercraft.'

Sarah Lister had tried in vain to persuade them to reduce their offer of 500 rides, having calculated that ten-minute trips for groups of sixteen would mean – with scarcely time for the change-overs – eight hours of continuous operation. Fortunately, their staff were highly organised, and had set up the day before a marquee with a cordoned area for queueing, preparations that proved invaluable when several hundred children began to arrive, many with parents, from early in the morning. There were far more than five hundred, and every one of them clutching a folder with the required pictures of Pepsi's cartoon heroes. It had very clearly been a successful promotion. Pepsi girls, with Hovercraft T-shirts, checked each album, and two more employees in super-hero costumes marshalled the kids into groups for each ride.

The children expressed their delight by skipping along the decking, others clenched their fists like goal-scoring footballers; the calmer ones stepped aboard the craft in wide-eyed wonder. They appeared to come from a fair cross-section of the income groups. With Peter Dixon leaving for the UK, it fell to Dick Bell to drive the craft, and he was just the man for the occasion. In England Dick spends much of his time leading holiday camps, loves to be surrounded by children and is remarkably gifted with them. His joy at giving so many children so much pleasure was obvious. He drove over Lake Managua on Pepsi Day, with only one short break, for nine hours. Night was closing in as the last of the trips was finishing.

The other major sponsors, Shell and Budget, decided to offer demonstration rides to their staff families. True to local culture, these became relaxed family outings rather than formal occasions. Spouses, chattering children and, quite often, aunts, uncles and ageing grandparents – all joined in!

Inviting on board a number of Government ministers and diplomats afforded an ideal opportunity to interview them about the project. Pablo Vijil, Minister of Transport and Communication, was very positive: 'We see an opportunity to open up areas of the country which have never, throughout all our history, been able to communicate with the developed areas. My first priority has been to build and maintain roads and ports, but few roads are economically feasible on the Atlantic coast. The area is scarcely populated, and in such isolated and low-lying terrain the cost of road building must be prohibitively high. The hovercraft could serve as a transport vehicle to river towns.' Focusing on the 'very important rain forest reserves' of the Río San Juan area, Minister Vijil welcomed the potential of hovercraft 'to travel through these waters without causing environmental damage.'

The British Ambassador was warmly in agreement with all that, but had been particularly struck by the calibre of the Steppers and younger hovercrafters. 'I have been very impressed with the hard physical work they've put in and their commitment to the Christian ideals behind the project. If this is typical of youngsters available from Britain, then let's have lots more of them!'

An assessment with a more controversial slant came from the senior official of the World Bank in Managua: 'It is so refreshing,' he said, 'to see these committed youngsters giving themselves to the poor of our country, without being cluttered with political dogma or weakened by considerations of political correctness.' It was heartening to hear an aid bureaucrat commending a project which, as we had already discovered, falls outside the officially prescribed development criteria. The banker was referring to the Europeans who poured into Nicaragua during the Sandinista era, bringing their ideological baggage. In recent years, as socialism has gone through radical review worldwide and the Nicaraguan revolution itself has faltered, they have quietly disappeared from the scene.

We took Pedro Chamorro, who had done so much for the project through *La Prensa*, together with his family, to the north-west corner of the lake. He explained that this spot, beneath the conical Momotombo volcano and close to the ruins of Old Leon, is the northern limit of Nicaragua's 'hydrographic axis' which so interested his father. It was therefore the furthest point north on the hovercraft's route across the country and its nearest point to the Pacific, which lies only a very few miles from Mount Momotombo. We knew that 'family' in Latin America would mean 'extended family' so were not at all surprised when he turned up with twelve: his wife, his sister, his sister-in-law and nine of their children. Pedro's eldest son, inevitably, carried the family name Pedro Joaquín. Mike realised that with the whole Chamorro dynasty, we had perhaps a sizeable proportion of Nicaragua's future leadership on board. He joked with Pedro about how the army, which has Sandinista tendencies, had nearly scrambled a helicopter a few days before to 'rescue' one of their generals. They had watched the Griffon cross the lake, and seen through binoculars that it was stationary, with passengers on deck. They assumed it had broken down; in fact the craft was resting on a sand bank and the party was enjoying a very rare opportunity of watching birds nest on a sandy island that few, if any of them, would have known existed, and which few, if any, could ever have visited before. They had radioed the general who was able to calm their fears and prevent them from pushing the panic button.

Crossing the lake one is able to look back at the Managua skyline, though 'skyline' is something of a misnomer since only four buildings break the horizon: Government House, the Intercontinental Hotel, the ruins of the old cathedral and Managua's new temple, the baseball stadium. We took the Chamorro family a trip of some fifty minutes across to the small island of Momotombito. It was, according to Pedro, a paradise for wild birds and other wildlife. It was therefore something of a surprise to hear the grunt of domestic pigs as we opened the hatches. But Pedro pointed up high into the tree branches crowded with large grey birds. 'We call them *patos chanchos* (pig-birds),' he explained, 'because of the noise they make.'

Although we only stayed a short while, the weather had

changed considerably by the time we began the return journey along the western shore of the lake. The wind had freshened and a sizeable swell developed, which first slapped, then crashed, against the hull. With the British Ambassador at the wheel, the rising sea and head wind combined to pull the craft 'below hump', and our speed fell to five knots. We sought shelter close in shore, and as the cabin lurched Mike made light of the situation by saying that the resilient Chamorro family would not have wanted an easy passage. Pedro probably realised that these were some of the most demanding conditions we had yet encountered. Finally Dick spotted, through the rain-lashed windscreen, a protruding sandbar which could be used to get back 'over hump'. He directed John Culver to head straight for it at full throttle, and as soon as we were over the sand the craft leapt forward and proceeded to scuttle over the swell at normal speed again. By the time we reached Managua, the storm had passed over and, as dusk fell, a wan sun shone briefly on the sodden waterfront.

In the twilight, Pedro's sister, Cristiana, spoke to our cameramen. Her opinions were significant not only because as Mrs Lacayo she is wife to the Prime Minister, but because of her passionate belief in her father's vision for the San Juan. 'My father described the San Juan as a lost paradise . . . I think it is important that you have gone to the river. If you can stay there you will help us rebuild that paradise, and the hovercraft will help to reunite Nicaragua.'

Her brother spoke with equal vigour in the lead editorial of the special supplement which *La Prensa* published that day entitled '*Misión Hovercraft*'. We had been pleased enough with two pages in the London *Times*; what were we to say of the twenty-four pages in Managua dedicated entirely to the project? Under the title '*Conquistadores Modernos*', Pedro wrote: 'The British have returned, this time not to conquer empires, but to conquer hearts with their Christian dedication . . . these *conquistadores* have declared war on indolence, on illness and on isolation. They are British heroes, but Nicaraguan heroes too. They merit our support.' Pedro also highlighted a feat which might have gone unnoticed. 'You have got thousands of Managuans to turn around and look towards the lake again.' Because of its pollution Managuans have turned their back on Lake Managua, and paid it little attention. 'Every Managuan on the Griffon,' he realised, 'had the unique experience of seeing their city from the water for the first time, a unique perspective which views the city as in a showcase. Only thus can we understand just how much the city has lost since the lake became so foul. Mike Cole and his team have challenged us to recover its lost resources.'

Pedro's enthusiasm was far from isolated. The supplement brought enthusiastic support in article after article, and advertisement after advertisement, all pouring out gratitude and goodwill. President Chamorro's Government took a full page to welcome this 'new era of friendship between Nicaragua and Great Britain'. The President herself was quoted: 'In the name of all my people I thank these friends led by Commander Cole who, together with Nicaraguans, have undertaken in their hearts this worthwhile task.' And the Mayor, Dr Alemán, not to be outdone, also took up a full page.

The tourist agencies were keen to make their presence felt. They recognised that with the appearance of the recently arrived hydrofoils from Belorussia and the hovercraft from Britain, the lake and the river could be offered as an important tourist route. One entrepreneur called for 'the re-conquest of the San Juan', and urged his fellow citizens to stand up to the tourism competition from neighbouring Costa Rica which has been increasingly prevalent on the San Juan in recent years. 'If the people of the river do not get their needs met in Nicaragua, they will look to the other side of the border,' the article argued. It was true; the team had seen it happening in Greytown. It had been happening for many years. The tourist agent insisted: 'When there's an undertaking that seems impossible, you need a visionary, strong in spirit, to take the first step; then others will follow with confidence. Such are our friends who have brought their hovercraft from Britain with such humanitarian goodwill. We could turn the San Juan, from today, into a source of employment, of income and of recreation. We have never been able to tackle the task before, but now, with the hydrofoils and the hovercraft, we have the tools to do the job.'

All this support from influential Nicaraguans was greatly encouraging. Mike's first response was to channel such a flood of local and national goodwill towards the British Government in the hope that it would help the fundraising battle. He sent copies of the President's message to John Major and to the Under-Secretary of State for the Americas at the Foreign Office, requesting an urgent re-examination of the funding application. 'We have taken this project as far as is possible on voluntary funding,' he wrote. 'Without some official support it will sadly be necessary to return the craft from the San Juan to the UK. The disappointment and let-down among Nicaraguans will be intense.' Mike was obviously well aware that the loans negotiated, being loans, in no way secured the project. He was also not best pleased when he heard that a visiting British official had let slip, at a reception where the wine had flowed fairly freely, that more official British aid money was being provided for prosperous Costa Rica than for impoverished Nicaragua. Such are the inconsistencies which political considerations impose upon official aid programmes. A few days later two faxes arrived, one sweet, one sour: a hearty note of congratulations from the UK patron Sir Edward Heath, and a polite but cold letter from the Foreign Office declining to review the decision!

In view of the premature end to the official reception, the Mayor kindly invited us to meet him in his office. Mike and Dennis accepted the invitation and found the Alcaldía a hive of activity. The impression given on the waterfront had been of a man able to talk the people's language and popular with many ordinary citizens. As we understood him to be a politician who would lead the country towards the right if elected to the Presidency, that was perhaps somewhat surprising. Most of the masses of Latin America would have other political preferences. Mike and Dennis were about to hear an anecdote that certainly would indicate Arnoldo Alemán had been no friend of the Sandinistas during the years of national turmoil.

163

The Mayor emerged himself to usher them into a modest office that spoke of a 'hands-on' operation rather than a distant executive role. The place exuded an aura of energetic activity and of power. They could not help but wonder if they were, in fact, in the presence of the next President of the Republic.

Dennis was to take the opportunity of handing over the last of his leather-bound Bibles. The Nicaraguan Bible Society had given the project six, one for the President herself and one each for the mayors through whose jurisdictions we would be passing. 'That's what we're here to do,' the Director of the Bible Society had said. 'To spread the Word of God among our people. Thank you for giving us the privilege.'

To many Latin Americans, even practising Roman Catholics, the Bible remains an unknown book, and many still confuse it with the missal. Dennis therefore was ready to recognise with some regret that these presentation copies might well remain, like many presentation Bibles, largely unused. Humanly speaking, it seemed to him especially unlikely that this burly, hyperactive, strong-man city mayor was going to find much time to scan the finer points of human life as outlined in the Bible. So he began in apologetic mood: 'I don't suppose, Señor Alcalde, that you have much time to read the Word of God. Are you at all familiar with it?' 'I certainly am!' came the surprising reponse. 'Some years ago I spent six months when it was the only book I had to read.' 'Really, how did that happen?' 'It was during the war. The Sandinistas put me in prison. When I asked for some reading material, they gave me the Bible and wouldn't let me have anything else. So I read it, and found it to be full of some wonderful wisdom. I often quote from it in my public speeches.' Finding good electioneering propaganda in the Word of God! 'Well,' Dennis thought to himself, 'I hope he might pick it up one day and find more than a few good "sound bites", for as millions of Latin America's new Bible Christians would say: Though needy feet need shoes; needy lives need Christ.' During that week of operations in Managua, Mike found time to get the team together in open forum on the subject of how best to develop the project. 'The Nicaraguans have left us with a remarkable opportunity,' he began, 'a blank sheet of paper to develop the project in any direction we choose. The limiting factor, for the moment, is financial; we can afford only a small-scale operation until September, so must concentrate on a few highly strategic objectives. To my mind, having shown the feasibility of a communication route, we must establish a reliable hovercraft service on the San Juan. That means fuel depots, ramps, turning circles and maintenance depots at suitable stages along the river.'

There were doubts in the minds of some about making this the priority, since the area that would be served was so very sparsely populated. Who would use – who would not be too poor to use – the service to be introduced? Mike listened and then defended his plans. He was attempting to view a longer-term strategy; he saw the need to make the San Juan more attractive and more accessible. It would not bring the immediate satisfaction of sick patients being cured, as trying to put a hoverdoctor service on to a populated river might have done, but it could revitalise an admittedly sparsely populated area and gradually become significant to thousands of people elsewhere in a variety of ways. He also felt himself committed to the river itself because that was where the Government had asked us to go.

He thought surveys of social needs in the Third World, however carefully observed and attractively presented, never did much to enthuse action. If, he believed, we could demonstrate what was possible, by action on the ground, Government officials, professionals and local people alike would know we were serious, would see the direction in which we were heading, and might well be persuaded to follow.

There were, he well knew, other needs that deserved attention. Some team members were keen to investigate more populated areas like the Punta Gorda river. Mike agreed to a few making the trek, but cautioned against imagining that a brief period of fact-finding was likely to yield development solutions.

Some months later he was pleased and excited to judge that his stance on the priorities was vindicated by a remark from

Carlos Coronel: 'All your excellent work around Bluefields certainly makes you a good Christian, but it doesn't make you a good politician.' And Carlos went on, whenever his favourite river was talked about, to declare with a confidence that would have rejoiced the heart of Pedro Joaquín Chamorro: 'The San Juan is the river of Nicaragua's future prosperity!'

There was no great team dissension. They came to see that concentration on the Río San Juan was not a decision against direct development work, but a vital first step towards longer-term effectiveness, and therefore of strategic importance from Mike's point of view.

But on one thing he insisted. The exploratory trip would have to be overland from Nueva Guinea. He was adamant that the hovercraft was not going to venture on to the ocean again until she had been more fully equipped for a sea operation, especially with a life raft. It was an expensive item, but it might be possible to send one out with the student top-up team. His main concern was not to over-extend the operation too soon, or risk a largely unpaid-for craft on an ocean that could easily turn ferocious in the rainy season which was now upon us.

As for the argument about ramps and turning circles, Gareth summed it up with characteristic pragmatism: 'It's all very well with twenty of you here to help me turn her around if the Griffon gets stuck, but when there are only a couple of us after September I'm really going to need them!'

Chapter 13

New Hope

Before the teams could get to work on establishing bases for hovercraft operations, there was some unfinished business in Managua. In the first place the craft had to return south, and there was no thought of taking it back through another 'Desert Storm'. It was hauled off the lake and loaded on to a truck for the first stage of its journey back to the San Juan.

There was also the small matter of a still enormous pile of medicines. Hardly a dent had been made in the donation by our small distributions in Bluefields, San Juan, Granada and elsewhere. Dr Ray, with Dennis in tow, worked hard at the Ministry of Health to find a home for the huge stock remaining. Officials were amazed at the quantity of stuff available, and expressed some surprise as to how it had come into the country. They said immediately that they would be unable to use anything that was out of date. Given that the makers insist their products are perfectly useful and entirely safe for many months after the official expiry date, this seemed a strange decision, and we were inclined to be critical. They explained: 'The press would murder us if they thought we were distributing out-of-date medicine!' It was understandable, but there was a bigger shock in store when, a few days later, they told us by phone that they would not be able to use any of it – too little time to get it distributed! It seemed a remarkable decision in a country where hospitals and clinics were crying out for resources of any sort; it was difficult to believe. Perhaps there were other factors at work.

We remembered the considerable surprise expressed when first they learnt about the consignment, and later we understood that the Ministry of Health must authorise the import of all medicines. Our special presidential decree had evidently by-passed the system; someone perhaps was sulking.

Be that as it may, it meant that immense quantities of drugs had to be disposed of usefully with the very minimum of delay. Incineration was as impossible as it was unthinkable. To be holding such a resource when surrounded by such a need should have made the task eminently simple; but we had to be careful. We could hand nothing over without a basic guarantee that a qualified professional would be responsible for prescribing. Finally a young Christian doctor appeared whose hospital, the Karl Marx, had been funded by the East Germans during the Sandinista regime. It was now being run under a scheme which charged the more affluent patients enough to subsidise the care of the indigent. Dr Ricardo opened up a vast, but largely empty, store, into which he delightedly put our sizeable contribution.

Ray discovered that lack of supplies was hindering the country's health services more than lack of qualified personnel. At first, we had felt ambivalent about the intrinsic rightness of a European firm unloading short-shelf-life stocks on the Third World, and had only calmed our consciences by the thought that no one could have envisaged Tiananmen Square. But when we saw the evident satisfaction on the faces of those who finally got those medicines, our qualms subsided.

We were also determined to catch up with the national Church leaders before we disappeared again into the remoter regions. The last hover on the lake was dedicated to Christian pastors and aid workers. But there was also the matter of bringing them together across the socio-political divide. Dennis organised a meeting in the project base, but with the time available it was not easy to publicise, and not many turned up. They did, however, represent different groups and Churches. Some were pastors from isolated areas in the far north who happened to be in Managua for a Bible Society event and had heard of our invitation. Those who came were fascinated by the story of what we were trying to do. There was a guitar, a violin and a time of Spanish worship. Dennis was able to share the word about forgiveness and reconciliation he had been wanting to share. He reminded them of the Genesis story of Joseph (Chapters 37–50), who was so desperately ill-treated by his brothers and suffered as a result for twenty-two long years in exile. Then, when God in his mercy brought them all together again, he managed to see God's hand in the whole sad story, and was able to hold nothing against them. The pastors went away with great satisfaction. They took quite a few gifts: bags of used clothes for their congregations, boxes of Christian literature for free distribution and study books for themselves. When they had no more hands and arms they carried boxes rural style on their heads, and as we watched them disappear down the road to catch their bus they reminded us of loaded Christmas trees!

The only other unfinished business in Managua was of a more light-hearted variety. The much anticipated cricket match, originally planned to greet our arrival in the capital, ended in a thorough defeat for the British. The carefree younger hovercrafters complacently allowed the other side to run up a reasonable score, then discovered that what the veterans of the Managua Cricket Club appeared to lack in physical fitness they more than made up for in bowling skill.

Mike left for a month in the UK to pursue fundraising. He had not yet given up on the ODA. Dick Bell also had to return to his UK commitments, so Mike delegated control of the Griffon to Gareth, who continued throughout 1995 and 1996 to make an outstanding contribution to the project. To operate comfortably the hovercraft would sooner or later need basic maintenance sheds and storing facilities in suitable locations. The more immediate need was for basic docking ramps, each with an associated circular area over which the craft could hover and turn, ready for its re-launch down the ramp at an efficient speed.

It was planned to provide these facilities in San Pancho, Greytown and Bluefields. Ian Coronel welcomed a group back to San Pancho with unstinting generosity. Since first the project had made contact with him, he had decided to stand for Congress in the 1996 election, as representative for the Río San Juan region. But that did not prevent him manning his small mechanical digger himself to work alongside the team as they laid a ramp on the river bank. At first he housed them in his guest rooms and, when these were in use, in the half-built buildings behind the house. He installed lighting and, when he began to realise how limitless was the supply of tinned curry, he brought in fresh fish from the river and meat from the farm, including venison! Mike had asked David Coates to head up the team that went to Greytown which, in fairness to modern-day Nicaragua, we ought to be calling San Juan del Norte. The 'Greytowners' – that was the problem: everyone found it easier to refer to them as that – were delighted to see them again, and housed them in the second of two schoolrooms which they had, as yet, no teacher to occupy. There were also plans to provide here, together with the hover base, a lodge. This aspect in particular had caught the imagination of Ambassador Culver, and he had found some funds to advance the project.

The Mayor marked his commitment by donating an ideal plot of land overlooking the river and under a shady canopy of trees. He had planned to build a home for himself there but now handed it over for a permanent Project Base. The Ambassador's financial contribution was specifically for living accommodation, and we judged his sense of priorities sound. San Juan was being seriously held back by the total lack of the most basic accommodation for visitors. It meant great difficulty in persuading even a development worker, much less a Government official or a Minister of State, to stay overnight. San Juan therefore remained largely unvisited by anyone of influence, and was consequently cut off from anyone who might assist in its development.

Matthew Falkiner carefully surveyed the site and returned upriver the next day to prepare detailed plans for a lodge to accommodate up to twelve people. These included a sizeable 'living-room' which could double up for use as a committee room for community leaders or for medical or agricultural

seminars. Matthew's plans were to make the standard of
the accommodation high enough, though rural, to attract
tourists as well as officials. Paying guests would provide a
small but worthwhile boost to the village economy. Matthew
had discovered that Greytowners in need of timber normally
cut it for themselves. He felt this was the most economical
way to meet the need. A muscular Creole called Fidel agreed
to provide all we required, free of charge, if we bought him
a chainsaw which he could keep for himself when the job
was over.

The team were not left idle when these plans and logistics
were being organised. They sweated to re-grade the river bank
ready for the ramp and basic turning circle. The sandy soil was
relatively easy to work, and though the ground was too soft
to permit a concrete base, a large slipway was completed in
a matter of days. The chainsaw arrived from Managua, and
Fidel disappeared with it into the jungle.

In San Pancho, however, the work was particularly exhausting, with climate the main factor. Progress was painfully slow,
and heat stroke affected some. Afternoons grew increasingly
wet, and the riverside mud was impossible to turn. It baked
hard again in the following morning's blazing sun, and proved
equally unyielding. The rain was refreshing enough, but it was
impossible to dig or mix cement with stair-rods of the stuff
falling on your back!

They resolved to get up in the dark in order to steal a
march on the weather. Journalists turned up one day from
El Nuevo Diario in Managua, trying belatedly to catch up with
their rivals at *La Prensa*, and were astonished to find shadowy
figures wielding pickaxes in the grey light of dawn. But this
schedule brought its own problems.

It left the team with too much leisure time in the heart of the
day. Things began to move slowly, like the herons standing at
the water's edge which only flapped their wings occasionally
to change their stance. Mike had promised that the time in the
jungle would be exacting; but neither he nor the team members
could have anticipated that each of them was going to have to
fight the toughest battle within. The adjustment to the pace of

life at San Pancho, and the determination to keep going on a mundane task in those tough conditions, had to be dragged up by each member individually from the depths of his or her own being.

At San Juan del Norte, while the team waited for timber to emerge from the forest, the same problem of lethargy arose. Volunteers were swapped between the two locations to bring some measure of variety but, perhaps surprisingly, most found it easier to be 'holed up' in San Juan than on the ranch upriver. Although the village was surrounded on three sides by jungle, and on the fourth by the ocean, it somehow felt less claustrophobic than San Pancho.

That was almost certainly due to the presence of a fascinating community of three hundred or more villagers, all vitally interested in the project. It made a difference. Bruce Howard showed commendable initiative in organising a children's adventure playground using jungle materials. The volunteers got on particularly well with the English-speaking Creoles, who often guided them into the dense jungle, padding barefoot at a phenomenal pace down slippery trails, and leaving their visitors panting and stumbling behind in high-tech walking boots! The guides carried rifles, to protect the group, so they said, from wild boar which had been known to attack humans. But in time the group came to suspect that the illicit drug smuggling rampant right along the coast was probably a more compelling reason. Drug running became a taboo subject, and it was thought best to make no comment on any unusual activity.

This greater sense of freedom at San Juan must also have owed something to the fact that some English was spoken. The contribution Steppers have made to Latin American situations has been incalculable, and their ability to communicate to youth across the cultures, while handling little or nothing of Spanish, never ceases to amaze those who watch. But language is an essential tool of human communication, and lack of it cannot but stifle human fellowship. Those who give themselves long-term to leave their mark – or rather, God's mark – upon another culture do well to pay due respect to the language, by learning to handle it well.

If tropical heat was one thing, windy afternoons were another. 'Your little house! Your little house! Come quick!' One of the maids at San Pancho was shouting in broken English as she ran up the path from the river. One tent had been pitched on a concrete patio overlooking the river, where the breeze made for a more comfortable night's sleep. The interlocking poles combined with the sleepers' weight kept the tent secure at night, but by day . . . Just in time, the girl had spotted the bright yellow mass bobbing down the river. A gust of wind during the afternoon rainstorm had lifted the fly-weight, poles and all, and dumped it unceremoniously in the San Juan. Iain Morris paddled after it in a precarious dugout, and managed to hook a protruding pole just before the whole mass sank beneath the water. He returned with his sodden bed, only to endure the usual team amusement!

Jungle survival, of course, presented its special challenges too. The mosquitoes at Greytown were ferocious but everyone learnt to recognise their preferred scavenging hours, covered up limbs and lit their repellent smoke coils. They had been in the habit of swimming regularly in the lagoon and in the tumbling surf before the locals congratulated them on their courage, and explained that sharks frequent both areas. Three years previously eighteen people from Bluefields were attacked when their boat turned over on the *barra*. And the team had blissfully taken a dip there back in May when waiting on the *Gloria* for the repaired Griffon to appear!

The ants had equally aggressive appetites. They peppered with holes the thick nylon groundsheets. So much for the reputation of this state-of-the-art equipment. At San Pancho snakes were a different and somewhat unexpected indignity. Where we had thought them more likely at San Juan, the cropped village grass frequented by people and animals was not as attractive to them as the long vegetation on the river just where they were building the ramp. There were several close calls with coral snakes, but, thankfully, no accidents. The farm workers insisted that any we met should be beaten to death, but when the Griffon engine was started on one occasion, there was some sympathy for the one that had gone to sleep coiled round the thrust fan!

Once Fidel had emerged from the jungle with a stock of wood, work began in earnest on the new lodge. Progress was determined by so many constantly shifting factors: bad weather, too few tools, a broken chainsaw, waiting for things to dry. The team learnt to measure their achievements over weeks, rather than day by day. The arrival of the top-up team from England brought a refreshing impetus to the hard slog on both sites. The newcomers often displayed more initiative than those who had been there throughout. In particular Rob McGregor revitalised the construction work at San Pancho. His hobby had been body-building, perhaps an unusual choice for a former fine art student. Just prior to joining the project he had suffered salmonella poisoning and had lost a staggering five stone in weight. He still weighed 168 pounds and had recovered sufficiently to make everyone else's efforts look puny! He was the perfect man to put in charge of concreting a huge area, thirteen metres by eight.

Friendship with the locals continued to make an important contribution to team morale at San Juan, and it was very much a two-way affair. One day several of the team helped to retrieve a fishing canoe capsized in the ocean breakers, when one of the fishermen had run to the village for help. A couple of the team bravely volunteered to swim out roped by the ankle, and Phil Adkins cracked his head on the semi-submerged boat as it swung violently in the waves. The locals roared with laughter, which not all the team thought entirely appropriate! But when men and dugout had been safely hauled ashore, and everyone was more relaxed, they came to realise that such light-heartedness in the face of danger and adversity was one more example of how locals defend themselves against the relentless hardness of life; they avoid, whenever they can, facing the realities head-on or with undue seriousness.

Among the last to arrive at Greytown were Matthew and Mark, a couple of RAF trainee fighter pilots, given leave to join the project while waiting for places on flying courses.

New Hope

Matthew made a valuable contribution, not by flying the Griffon, as might have been imagined, but by confidently taking control of a couple of monstrous lobsters and turning them into a delicious meal for the team. His father had once owned a fish shop! The lobster-fishing season from August to October brings to the men of San Juan a brief, risky but highly lucrative occupation. They can earn hundreds of dollars, if all goes well, selling lobsters in Costa Rican ports.

David Coates came across an example of the cultural divide on the Atlantic coast itself when he visited a maize plantation run by one of the Hispanics. The planter was highly frustrated that his attempts to form a farming co-operative had been opposed by those he saw as 'boozing fishermen'. Mark, with his RAF background, was reminded of the aircrew/ground-crew divide, the reckless fishermen being the cocky pilots, and the steady farmers the thorough ground mechanics.

The hovercraft itself, of course, was active throughout all these months, and Gareth undoubtedly the busiest team member. He did his best to develop the piloting skills of others, but inevitably most of it had to be done by him. Dick and Peter, before returning to the UK, had given tuition to team members on Lake Managua. With nothing else afloat it was an ideal place for novice drivers. Dick used to urge his pupils to 'fly by the seat of their pants', throw the controls around and 'get the feel'. Peter gave detailed instructions on the how and the why of each control, and urged gentle movement. Presumably these styles reflected their own flying experience, Dick as the fast Lightning jet pilot, Peter at the controls of heavy-lift Hercules cargo planes. These sessions would ultimately have to be replaced by similar ones training those who were going to be responsible long-term for the operation of the craft. Nationals would need to be trained.

But meanwhile Gareth faced his responsibility with the Griffon doggedly and cheerfully, completing a punishing schedule that combined supply trips with numerous excursions for visitors and officials. They were not always straightforward journeys, but each eventuality led to a better-equipped and better-prepared service for the future.

175

On one occasion on a trip upriver, the engine cut out suddenly and the craft began to float slowly backwards towards the rapids, the anchor proving inadequate in the alluvial river bed. They had to make a long line out of every piece of rope on board, and were about to swim it to the bank, when – incredibly – a dugout appeared on an otherwise empty river. The line was taken, anchored firmly to a tree, and the drift towards the rapids was arrested. The fault was merely a jammed fuel gauge; they had run out of diesel. There was, of course, a reserve supply on board but the incident, which could well have resulted in serious damage, underlined the need to add something to the equipment carried – perhaps a grappling hook – so as to be ready for every eventuality.

A number of influential Nicaraguans took advantage of the new hydrofoil service, by then working across Lake Nicaragua, to join the hovercraft on the river. But it was Gareth's care of the more humble officials, teachers, health workers and representatives from the Mayor's office, that proved the most satisfying. The craft was beginning to assist those who were doing most for the development of the region.

Involvement with the Christian community in San Juan was a significant part of the team's rich experience there, and they had every reason to be pleased at having caused the renewal of activities in the little church. The abandoned building, seen on the 1994 recce, had remained closed and dank. It had been built some years previously with the help of some Americans but, for reasons which the team failed to uncover, the congregation had gradually dwindled and services had ceased. It was not a promising situation, but one Sunday the team invited the lay pastor's wife – her husband was away travelling – to open up the building. It was a small and inauspicious beginning. When the pastor returned, he warmed to the idea of re-introducing regular services. Villagers were drawn in, doubtless some from curiosity at the presence of the *gringos*, and considerable interest was generated at an open-air service to which team members contributed song and drama. It seemed likely that without further help the enthusiasm would wane after their departure. David Coates was to be all the more thrilled

An exuberant welcome on arrival in Managua.

The Mayor of Managua, Dr Arnoldo Alemán
(now President Elect), receives the team on the *malecón*.

Managua: the team share in the celebration.

Dick Bell drove for nine hours, giving
800 youngsters hover experience.

Victoria Sinclair and Harold Briley: team members young and
not-so-young enjoy Pepsi day.

Pedro Joaquín Chamorro views the
special hovercraft edition of *La Prensa*.

The street kids are quite cheeky.

Dreaming of a better future on the Mosquito Shore.

The lodge at Greytown built by Steppers.

Young STEP volunteers delivered to Greytown by hovercraft.

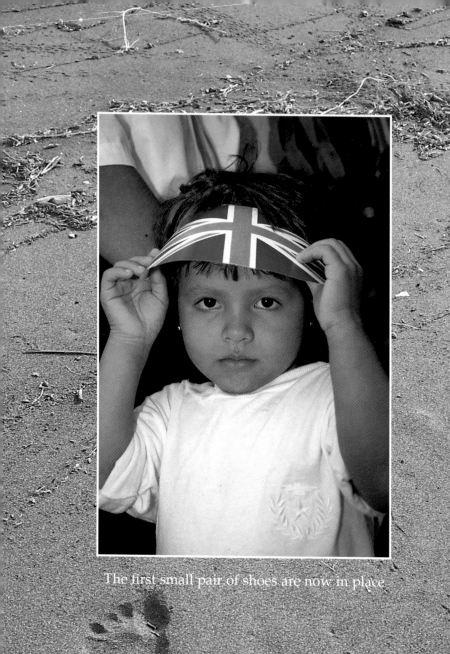

The first small pair of shoes are now in place

therefore when, a year later, he discovered the congregation flourishing, and the little church in regular use.

In the medical field Ray set out, with the help of Matthew Dixon, to survey the health needs of every home in San Juan. She spoke at length to Lionel, a Costa Rican who acts as village nurse for four months every year, and spends the rest of the time with his family in San Carlos. He saw lack of medicines as the greatest issue, along with the infrequency of visits by a doctor or medical brigade, because of totally unpredictable river transport. Lionel went down the river at least once by hovercraft and was thrilled at its potential.

Before she left the country, Ray went on to produce a comprehensive survey of the situation prevailing in the whole of the southern Atlantic area, and her considered opinion was that the five greatest needs in order of priority were:

AFFORDABLE TRANSPORT
GOOD WATER SUPPLY & SANITATION
MEDICINES
IMPROVED DIET with special advice on pig-breeding
MEDICAL PERSONNEL

From her very considerable experience in the medicine of poverty she recommended that we investigate ways in which the hovercraft could be put at the disposal of the activities of those agencies already in existence. A study should be undertaken of how its use could be co-ordinated, and personnel trained for its operation and maintenance.

Of such agencies there are a number. One which had come to our attention early on was Acción Médica Cristiana (Christian Medical Action), a volunteer group forged on the campus of Managua University during the days of turmoil. Evangelical students were coming together around their new-found faith in a student Christian Union, and were moved by the need of their country in the aftermath of natural disasters, especially in the more remote areas. Medical students, together with one or two graduate doctors and nurses, then did something that has been all too rare in Latin American history. They put their own comfort to one side and formed self-help *brigadas* to pay short-term visits to needy areas in their holiday periods – a sort of indigenous STEP movement! By now, with the help of a few committed professionals, that movement has become a duly incorporated, non-profit-making organisation with premises in Managua and a very significant programme of outreach. AMC operates three high-speed *pangas* for five days a week; the Griffon could quite obviously greatly extend the scope of what they are doing.

Yet when young leaders of AMC in Managua were pressed to say what they considered the organisation's greatest need, they did not mention doctors, nurses, medicines or hovercraft. It was Bible teachers they asked for! Why Bible teachers if they were doing social and medical work? 'Because,' they said with conviction, 'we ourselves would never have done anything for our country if it had not been for the Bible. We would have found a job, or put up our brass plates in Managua to do what professionals are expected to do. It was God's Word that opened our eyes, our hearts and our pockets. Unless you send us Bible teachers, the University Christian Union that brought us into being may wither and die!' Bible teachers were not, of course, something that the British hovercraft team could, of itself, provide. Bible teaching in cross-cultural situations is a life's work, a long-term activity. But Latin Link in London will certainly have noted the unexpected request; it is their forte.

The team did, of course, come across medical emergencies. A badly wounded man was brought in one day, having been carried for six hours through the jungle. He had been involved, three days before, in a machete fight, and had been losing blood ever since. Ray cleaned out a leg wound but decided that the local treatment of putting ground coffee into wounds to reduce the bleeding was reasonably effective, so she left his head wound alone. He was taken by *panga* into Costa Rica. As usual it was impossible to find out the cause of the quarrel; it could have been the Creole–Hispanic divide, a settling of old war scores, or perhaps a drug feud.

On another occasion a fourteen-year-old girl was in difficult labour, and her life was undoubtedly saved when she was hovered upriver to San Carlos. And an elderly couple who had been stuck there for sixteen days after a surgical operation, and were quite unable to pay for the river trip home, were taken back to Greytown. The little church suggested a collection afterwards to pay the project the 'fare'. In the face of such poverty, one's heart would have wanted to turn the offer down, but it is important that Third World Christians be encouraged to help themselves, even if their contribution is but token-sized. The matter highlighted the relevance of the team's doubts about who would be able to afford to use a hovercraft service if one were regularly available. Was it always going to depend upon a foreign subsidy? The self-help support of the Nicaraguan Churches ought perhaps to become at least a part of the answer to that problem. The marketing of vegetables grown in remote areas and the efficient rearing of pigs are two pressing agricultural problems. Team members Rob Babington-Smith and Amanda Miller volunteered to stay on in Nicaragua to develop such self-help schemes.

When Mike returned from the UK he was able to give the go-ahead to extend operations northwards along the coast. He also brought the good news that the Trust in London had turned £25,000 of their loan into an outright gift. (Later this gift was increased to £50,000.)

With the concrete ramp complete at San Pancho, and the basic structure and roof in place at the San Juan Lodge, the centre of operations moved north to Bluefields, where Jonathan Allan and John Green had gone ahead to make arrangements for the construction of a third slipway and of the hovercraft's maintenance garage. The plan was to combine more ramp work with hovercraft excursions to explore the coast and rivers on either side of the town.

Members had a choice of how to get themselves north from San Juan. Those who hovered straight down the coast enjoyed the best of journeys at an excellent speed and in fine weather. Four members decided to walk it! David Coates was one of them. He writes:

'The ultimate challenge had been in our minds for some

time. To walk the one hundred miles up Nicaragua's Caribbean coast from Greytown to Bluefields. Few locals have ever done it. We had no idea how easy or difficult the journey would prove, but set out early one moonlit night, keen to cover as much ground as possible by daybreak. There were four of us, Mark (the RAF flight lieutenant), Chris, Vicky and myself. We trudged silently through the soft sand, tingling with excitement at the prospect of the impending adventure.

'Reaching the coconut plantation at Cangruera we flicked on our torches to display our presence rather than have some trigger-happy soldier open fire. The army maintains its presence through this drug-smuggling area. But no one challenged us.

'Chris took up a fierce pace, swinging his machete like a warrior in battle. I muttered something about having another forty hours to go, and we slowed to about three miles an hour. We passed a deserted village, eerie in the moonlight; many must have perished there in the recent fighting. We needed a well but feared stirring up stray dogs, so gave the place a wide berth, and made do with what water we had. Rejoining the beach the going became easier over hard sand. First one wreck, then another, loomed up out of the darkness – fishing vessels run aground and long since abandoned. Their spectres added to our intense sense of loneliness.

'At Spanish Creek we faced a dilemma. Cross the strong current or go upstream where the river was shallower but wider? We considered waiting until daylight, and I groaned under the responsibility of making the decision. "There's only one way to find out," said Chris, and dived in. We held our breath. He ended up opposite us on the far bank, though he had been swimming diagonally against the current. He crossed back over and, after tying our ankles to a makeshift raft on which we put the rucksacks, we splashed and swam our way across, immensely relieved to be safe. A local man delighted in telling us that sharks often venture upstream when rivers

180

are in flood. He warned us to check for small cuts, since blood was an open invitation.

'We stood dripping on the other side of the creek, the sandflies driving us to distraction. Hurrying off barefoot we suddenly realised the machete was missing. We could not do without it, so Chris and I trotted back and, after a few anxious minutes and another swim, happily retrieved the invaluable tool. It was four in the morning and we were asleep on our feet. Dawn was long in coming.

'Suddenly torchlights appeared from the edge of the jungle, so we quickly lit ours. They grew closer and some kind of confrontation was clearly inevitable. The shadowy figures were almost upon us when we recognised one as a certain Carlos whom we had met in San Juan. He and his friends had been trying to get some sleep in a makeshift shelter, but it was proving impossible: "No sleep, plenny fly!" was their verdict. We realised some explanation on our part was necessary, so I stated our ambitious plan to reach Bluefields. We needed a guide. Would someone be willing to take us on to Punta Gorda? Carlos pondered this problem so long I wondered if he had heard me. Eventually we were introduced to Alfredo, who vanished into the darkness to collect his belongings.

'The sun was up and already very hot by the time we reached Corn River. Only eight houses. We flopped exhausted on to the floor of a rough shelter used as a Catholic church. It had taken us eleven hours to complete the first thirty miles of our marathon. We dozed on and off during the day through the increasing heat, and arranged to leave at midnight, now with two guides, Alfredo and his cousin Manuel.

'It was raining when we got up and, as we filled our bottles from the rain cascading off the roof, we pondered how many miles lay ahead. We waited a very long time for the guides to find a boat but were shaken wide awake when crossing the Corn River in a desperately unstable dugout in total darkness. We strode off along the beach, and stopped two hours later at Punta Roca, a fearsomely rocky headland, unable to go further since it meant entering the jungle in darkness, and even our guides were unwilling to do that. To the delight of the sandflies we had to doze fitfully under banana leaves to wait for daylight.

'Dawn came and we splashed across another creek before plunging into the jungle. We were climbing sharply. These were the *montes* we had heard so much about, home of the *chanchos de montes*, the wild boar that hunt in packs and surround their prey before attacking. We stuck together, stomping clumsily after our bare-footed guides. Would we ever reach Punta Gorda? The route was impossibly tortuous and needed every kind of contortion as we slithered over rocks and squirmed through creepers and past trees with vicious spikes. Previous jungle experience paled into insignificance as we waded uncertainly through waste-deep swamps, slapping continuously at the relentless mosquitoes. Manuel once called a halt as he thought he "smelt a snake". With anonymous creatures plopping into the stinking mess all around us, this came as no surprise! But I was in no mood to stop.

'Every so often we would emerge on to a beach of breath-taking beauty. But we were by now filthy and exhausted, and could only collapse under the nearest coconut tree to gorge ourselves on its milk, and munch mechanically through stale bread rolls and tuna fish, glad of every scrap of food we had brought.

'After thirteen hours of the second day my left leg gave up as we waded along the banks of the Punta Gorda river towards another borrowed dugout. I felt I couldn't continue, and almost resigned myself to the thought of a rest day that we could ill afford. Vicky, who never appeared to suffer any ill-effects, was a great encouragement in her quiet, unassuming way.

'We gratefully spent the night on the floor of one of the only three rough wooden homes on that vast estuary. Mother had broken her arm years before and, being far from medical help of any sort, it had reset itself grotesquely. Father looked the worse for wear and in need of several good baths. Before settling to sleep, I cautiously eyed enormous spiders hanging dangerously from the palm roof.

'We rose at four, and were immediately wading across another infernal creek, any hope of keeping our feet dry immediately dashed. Moreover my right boot upper was separating from its sole, and large amounts of packing tape were necessary to keep the two parts in harmony. Swamps and packing tape don't work well together, and the whole thing soon became a sorry mess. By the time we had wound our way back along the northern bank of the Punta Gorda, dawn was breaking, and my sole was flapping again against the sand. It took us six hours to reach Monkey Point and, very weary, I clung to two simple thoughts: that every step took us nearer our goal, and I didn't have to walk back!

'In the baking midday heat we sank heavily on to the dirt floor of a little village "shop", kicked off our soggy boots, and enjoyed the most delicious bananas we ever expect to taste. The socks dried within minutes to the consistency of stiff cardboard. I bought some rice, and turned meekly to ask the girl if she might cook it for us.

'The beach was inviting, but pulling on boots and piling on the suncream we set off doggedly again inland. It was very hot, and we were eager to get back to the beach by nightfall. Our aim was to leave just the walk up the sand – about twenty-five miles – for the last day. We walked through maize fields and grass so high that we couldn't see over it. We picked our way along cliff edges, and slowly across the rocks and through the surf. I was more dirty and smelly than I had ever been before, but quite beyond caring. The sun grew steadily more golden as we finally arrived back on the beach. No more jungle, no more swamps and no more cliffs. Just sand, sand and more sand. Our spirits soared dramatically.

'But the last night of the journey was more uncomfortable than either of the previous two. The guides appeared vaguely acquainted with the inhabitants. We were led to something resembling a well, where we made a feeble attempt to wash, using half a bucket between us. And then we supped on cold curry and avocado. But sharing one's pallet with dogs and chickens is no recipe for sleep. When at last I thought I'd managed it, a brute of a hen pecked my big toe, and I sat bolt upright banging my head on the table under which I was lying. Children's crying and mother's vituperative Creole continued long into the night, and by the time all the fuss had died down it was time to be moving off down the beach. We were glad to get away from the place.

'As dawn came I tried to imagine myself doing anything other than walking along that endless beach. Islands had appeared far ahead on the horizon; we studied the map. It seemed impossible that we should have to draw level with these tiny shapes and leave them far behind us before we could reach Honson Point. We finished the last of our food, and only the thought that our ordeal was nearly over persuaded us to carry on. As in a trance we came upon fishermen catching crabs in the shallows, and the skipper agreed to take us to Bluefields – for a price. It was our only hope and I was elated! We had walked as far up the coast as possible, and there were no other boats in sight. All that was required of us was to wait once more. We threw ourselves down on the sand as though we should never rise again. It was 7.40 a.m. on Saturday, 12 August. We had walked nearly a hundred miles in three and a half days, completing a journey that few, if any, white people have ever done before.

'Three hours later, squashed between crates of dying crabs, we chugged into Bluefields, disembarked and stumbled anonymously up the jetty and into the town.'

Another group got to Bluefields the long way round: up the San Juan, across the lake by hydrofoil, bus to El Rama via

Managua, and river boat to Bluefields – some five times further than David and his friends had had to walk. They had their adventure too. While waiting on the quay at El Rama a group of six were casually watching a truck being unloaded. Among its cargo was a large number of cylinders of propane gas for cooking. Alan Blake will always remember what happened next: 'Suddenly we heard a terrific explosion and, as in a war film, two men were literally blown off the back of the truck and flames started to shoot out of the gas bottles. As the two men got up and sprinted away, it took a few seconds to realise the seriousness of the situation. Gas cylinders began to be hurled through the air, and pieces of timber were falling close to us. It was too late to run so we jumped into the river and clung to the tyres which served as bumpers along the pontoon side, with only head and shoulders above water. But debris was still falling so we swam further downriver. Eventually the fire died down and we ventured back to our kit which we had abandoned on the quayside. Only after the danger had passed did the full force of what had happened hit me, and I felt physically sick with the shock of it.'

Though shaken none of the party was harmed. The hovercraft team regrouped in Bluefields just as the Steppers were coming to the end of their time there. They had completed the main structure of the second classroom block; only the fitting of windows and doors remained.

The wet season delayed its appearance, so good progress was made on the concrete base for the main hovercraft garage. Earthmovers from the timber yard quickly levelled a wide turning circle and a site for the building itself. The Steppers had also done much to revitalise the Verbo congregation in the town, and encourage Pastor Ed. The nature of the STEP team's relationship with this gentle pastor and his family was displayed one sultry afternoon when Ligia was out shopping, together with some of the team.

'*Ladrón! Ladrón!*' she shrieked, and the bag-snatcher was a hundred yards away before she remembered to change to 'Thief! Thief!' Nigel, hampered by mud-caked wellies, gave chase, and brought the scoundrel down in a rugby tackle.

When Ligia arrived she recognised her fishmonger, and in one voice they exclaimed to each other incredulously: 'You!' The police arrived, and the thief was sentenced to do time in gaol, one week to one year, the length to be determined by the victim. Compassion prevailed, and he got seven days. The church was glad to see him attend the Sunday service they hold in the prison each week!

The time had come to organise, concurrently with the building work, a programme of exploration so that we could begin to determine how the Griffon could best serve the area. The team divided into two, and took turns working on site and crewing the various river trips. The first foray was north to visit two villages on Pearl Lagoon. At Orinoco the friendly Creole villagers sold them a huge basketful of freshly cooked shrimps for just a few *córdobas*. Suddenly there was less interest in hovercraft driving lessons. Everyone wanted to be sitting in the main cabin shelling the delicious prawns.

On the following day the Griffon went south for two hours to arrive at the mouth of the Río Punta Gorda. The river was reasonably wide, but after fifty minutes it narrowed as we passed the settlement of Atlanta. Several figures gesticulated to us wildly to stop – there were impassable rapids ahead. We pressed on, coasting easily over the shallows although the river was now closing in on all sides. After fifteen minutes we reached the village of Número Uno. It was a community which had been visited earlier, in response to Mike's permission for an overland trek of discovery. It had taken two full days from Managua, a day by road followed by a day of canoeing and driving, with a final seven-hour hike through the jungle. Now we had arrived in one morning from Bluefields. Despite the name – Number One – there was really nothing first-class about the place. The settlement was bleak, its people sullen. It seemed that most of the men were former Sandinista fighters who had been resettled there by the Government. Though not unwelcoming, the atmosphere did contrast sharply with the cheerful outlook of the Creole villagers at San Juan and at Pearl Lagoon. Despite its unprepossessing feel we decided to write Número Uno into our long-term development plans.

186

On the Sunday we visited Rama Kay at the southern end of Bluefields Bay, and attended a morning service at the Moravian church there. It was remarkable to enter into the heritage of the early European missionaries who had taken their Moody and Sankey hymnbooks with them. They were still in enthusiastic use, and the church in that remote spot was packed with people. Afterwards the local school teacher explained that the last Miskito king, one Robert Clarence (the kings were established by the British during the Protectorate period), had had links with Rama Kay. They were anxious to find out everything they could about their history, primarily, it seemed, in order to prove their title to lands on a nearby shore that, they claimed, was being settled illegally by Nicaraguans (*sic*) from across the forest! The longstanding divide is as sharp as ever.

There was time for just one more exploratory trip, to the Río Grande, as far north of Bluefields as Greytown is to the south. Ray Pinniger had learnt from health officials that some eighteen thousand people live in fifty settlements along the river. They left at 7 o'clock one morning, and after a brief stop for a shrimp breakfast at Orinoco reached the top of the Pearl Lagoon after two and a half hours. Then to the broad current of the Río Grande, where they hovered upriver for about half an hour before realising that they were not going to reach the main settlement of La Cruz del Río and still get back by dark. But this remotest of regions needed just a two-day trip. On the way back they paused at the village of La Barra on the northern bank, a community of a hundred people with no medical service at all, and took Jessica, a sick girl, and her grandmother back to Bluefields. Three hours later the two were on Bluefields quay, just a small act of kindness that we hope will continue to mark the developing hovercraft ministry.

On the final day we were privileged to see the Griffon being used professionally with another development agency for the first time. Two Nicaraguans working for the American NGO Auxilio Mundial, or World Relief, flew into Bluefields from Managua, and Gareth took them down to Número Uno on the Punta Gorda river. They gathered the information they needed for a project funding proposal, and were thrilled to be back in Bluefields the same day. We were thrilled too to see the craft's potential as a communication tool being successfully tapped at this early stage. If Ray's recommendation was to be followed up, this was the model of partnership that could be extended across a variety of organisations, widening and deepening the help being given to our new-found friends on Nicaragua's Mosquito Shore.

*   *   *   *   *

The time had come for almost all of the volunteers to leave. Some would be coming back to their studies, some to face their fresher year in university, others to take another step in their career structures. Peter Dixon came back to command his University Air Squadron, Dick Bell to plan his children's camps and Christian conferences. Areas of uncertainty remained, not least the financial one. Mike would be commuting between Nicaragua and the UK for some time to come in an effort to resolve it. Some had more time to give and worked on overseas.

But some glorious certainties remained too. A flame of concern had been lit in the UK for the welfare of a nation that has suffered too much, whose naked feet deserve more than a small pair of sandals. Ken Pollard, for example, returned to Scunthorpe, and to that group – who trekked all over the fells of Cumbria to finance themselves in 1996 – the project owes the completion of the school at Bluefields. The flame of concern is likely to go on burning brightly and, hopefully, to spread.

And for the Atlantic coast of Nicaragua there exists, undeniably, new hope. Mosquitia is awakening, and if the project's contribution to that revival had been but a very small one, it would still be Mike Cole's supreme satisfaction, and the satisfaction of all who supported him.

Epilogue

Since the journey was completed the project has surged ahead on a broad front.

The volunteer team from Scunthorpe that saw the third stage of the school construction completed at Bluefields went to Gatwick with a cement mixer, and took it to Managua as checked passenger baggage with Continental Airlines. First Nick Case-Green with the Griffon fan, now Ken Pollard with a cement mixer! We gladly acknowledge the highly supportive commitment of Continental Airlines to the project.

The hurricane season brought its threats to the building programme and to team safety. But withdrawal was apparently not in anyone's mind as Hurricane Caesar headed towards them across the Caribbean. They had built a septic tank which, happily, had not yet been put into use, and in this they prepared to spend the night. At the last moment Caesar, as hurricanes tend to do, changed direction and only its angry edge touched Bluefields.

Despite persistent torrential rain Ambassador Culver attended the school's inauguration. The mud was horrendous, and he returned to the capital bespattered, having witnessed the successful culmination of a plan first mooted three years before. Both he and Mike were filled with admiration for the team's work. The construction has given a new dimension to Bluefielders' plans for their Verbo school; opening a Secondary Department of their own is now on the agenda.

'Aren't we ever going to see you again, Mike?' asked Pastor

Ed as the inauguration came to an end, and the team prepared to leave. 'We've come to appreciate you all so much and the relationship we share. We love you, Mr Mike.' Mike was sure future developments would give many opportunities of renewing friendship. Though not much given to shows of emotion he must have felt the lump in his throat when he admitted that the sense of bereavement was going to be mutual.

In London, All Souls is that beautiful Nash church in Langham Place at the head of Regent Street, hard beside the BBC building. The fashionable congregation run a 'Wetfoot' programme (not unlike STEP) for those who want to dip their toes into Third World realities. The team that David Coates recruited – Brenda Muckley from *The Times* went with them too – did rather more than dip their toes into Nicaragua. Starting in Los Brasiles outside Managua, they added a much needed kitchen to the orphange premises, and then moved down the San Juan to Greytown. A UK charity loaded them with 750 teddy-bears, which they enjoyed distributing. They also financed the purchase of 400 study books in Spanish for use by Nicaraguan pastors and Christian leaders. So many are the needs, so great the opportunities to serve.

A third team went to Juigalpa on the road from Managua to San Carlos, where they added to the construction of a community and agricultural research centre. Mike took them in the Griffon down the river to Greytown too. In fact, inadvertently, he took them a little further. They had been delayed before setting out, and by the time they got to the lower reaches of the river night had fallen. At the tricky section where the river meets the sea they suddenly hovered into fog, and after some effort to find the channel which leads to the village, realised they were in fact heading out across the Caribbean! They turned, but the channel into Greytown was far from obvious, and the situation became a little tense. Then the villagers, hearing the Griffon passing to and fro, recognised what had happened and came out of their homes en bloc, waving lighted wicks and torches to guide the Griffon home. In spite of the uncomfortable moments, Mike was delighted that the villagers had been given this opportunity of showing their concern and solidarity; the Griffon was already important to Greytown and when she was in trouble the whole town had come unitedly to her rescue.

David Coates has given himself to the people there, not just as an administrator of a communication service but as a friend and counsellor, and they have taken him to their hearts. Perhaps the now distant and tenuous links which England has had with the Mosquito Shore have made it easier for them to welcome him, and for him, and us, to feel at home with them. Three years ago the British Ambassador said that we would find it so.

Greytown is resurgent. The village school functions encouragingly, with a newly appointed head teacher from Managua. Concrete paths of access have been laid and there are plans to give the village a simple focal point. The twelve-bedded lodge that Matthew Falkiner designed is an exceptional building for its location. The British Ambassador was present at the inauguration, and highly delighted with what he saw. But what made the day altogether memorable for the locals was the presence of three Nicaraguan Cabinet ministers. Aldrick, on whose floor we had slept in 1994, nudged Mike in the ribs as he contemplated the scene. 'We've never seen one before,' he said, 'and look, you've brought us three all together!' The lodge has since been in steady demand, and a local inhabitant has been given the job of caring for the place and administering the bookings. With leading figures now able to visit from elsewhere in the country, and stay the night, San Juan del Norte has been lifted on to a new plane.

When a telephone engineer visited from Managua, the extent of progress was graphically illustrated. 'There's been total stagnation here since before the war, but we shall be able to leapfrog the technology now,' he explained. 'No need to bother with installing landlines. We shall go straight to the radio phone!' He was already planning the installation of the necessary equipment. Could just one craft have achieved so much in such a short space of time? Two years ago Greytown was a settlement with two names, four cemeteries and a past. Now it was on the way to becoming a place with a future.

Perhaps the most significant development of all is that the Nicaraguan route between the oceans, with which this book opened, has now broken again on to the international scene. Because many modern vessels are too large for the Panama Canal, a rail link across Nicaragua, with container facilities, is being considered as an alternative route for the 21st century. An international consortium based in the Far East has signed a contract for a feasibility study to construct a 'dry canal' from Monkey Point on the Caribbean to Corinto on the Pacific. The modern 'industrial gold rush' is thrusting the Nicaraguan canal back into world attention. Though unlikely to happen immediately, such a development would, of course, give hope to the whole country, and especially to that jungle coastline through which David and his friends made their epic walk. There are so many ways in which the presence of hovercraft in such a water-dominated area could complement and enhance the railway link. We shall watch developments with intense interest.

Meanwhile, we do not expect a telephone link, a regular passenger service or twelve beds available in a lodge to resolve of themselves the human needs we met in San Juan del Norte. The problems of life are much too deeply seated to be affected by such material improvements. But all has been done in the name of Christ and as an expression of Christ's love for the people of the Mosquito Shore. And our conviction is that he has the answer to all human need.

The Griffon has been used on several occasions as an emergency ambulance, but there are no immediate plans to establish a hover-borne medical service of our own. The craft will be put at the disposal of other medical aid programmes so as to extend the scope of the services they already provide.

One of the most exciting of these is the Smiley Campaign. Every year this imaginative US-based project sends a volunteer plastic surgeon, with his own medical team, to the Granada hospital, for the sole purpose of repairing as many hare-lips and cleft palates as possible, using a caring but 'conveyor-belt' approach to the operation. Remembering the desperate lack of facilities in that Granada hospital, we were glad to know that the team bring with them all the equipment they need.

For some reason not entirely understood, a great many Central American children are born with such disfigurement, some more serious than others. It is, of course, much more than a cosmetic problem, endangering general health and impeding development both physically and emotionally. So the work of the Smiley Campaign puts much more than a visible smile on the face of its patients.

But such has been its success over the years that many of the most serious cases have already been treated. Families living in inaccessible places, however, have never heard of the Smiley offer, and if they were to hear would still be quite unable to reach Granada. So the hope is that the campaign could use the hovercraft to identify and collect isolated patients currently beyond the reach of this wonderfully effective US programme.

*　*　*　*　*

Mike Cole calculated the risks when he gave the go-ahead for a capital-heavy project without the certain backing of adequate sponsorship. He saw the prize to be gained as worth the risk to be taken and did not expect God to fail him. Having seen what has already been accomplished he does not expect God to fail him now. But the whole programme has been sustained by voluntary effort on relatively small donations, and although some two-thirds of project costs have already been raised, if the Griffon is to stay and serve the people of Nicaragua, £200,000 is urgently needed; the Griffon is not yet totally paid for and there are interest-free loans still to be repaid. To bring the craft back to Britain, and destroy the expectations that have been raised in Nicaragua, would be tragic and, to those most closely involved, unthinkable.

We speak for ourselves and may be biased, so we shall give the last word to someone else. The following was received from the Nicaraguan Minister of Transport as this book was going to press:

Gobierno de Nicaragua
Ministerio de Construcción y Transporte

Despacho del Ministro

Managua,
13th September, 1996

Dear Mr. Cole,

I am writing this letter to thank you and your colleagues who took care of us during our trip to Greytown. For me it was a beautiful experience, a first, in that remote part of our territory which I had only seen from the air before.

Your determination in accomplishing the goals set a few years ago, is bringing many benefits to our land. In particular the poor communities along the Rio San Juan and South Atlantic coast. I cannot express in words all my appreciation to your efforts on behalf of Nicaragua.

I hope that this great effort will continue and expand to other isolated communities along the rivers of the Nicaraguan Atlantic coast. Our country is striving to overcome extreme poverty and the co-operation of good friends like you will be forever appreciated.

Best Regards,

Pablo Vijil Ycaza

Minister of Construction and Transport

Appendix A

Glossary of Spanish Words

abajo	down
Acción Médica Cristiana	Christian Medical Action
agua	water
albergue	a lodge
alcalde	a mayor
alcaldía	the mayor's office
antisomocista	an opponent of the Somoza regime
aquí	here
arriba	up
Auxilio Mundial	World Aid
bala	an ancient weapon for de-rigging schooners
barra	a sandbar at the mouth of a river
brigada	a brigade (often of para-medical personnel)
campesino	a peasant
canción	a song
castillo	a castle; fort
CEPAD	Spanish acronym for: Evangelical Committee for Emergency Aid
chamba	a fluke
chancho	a pig
colegio	a secondary school
colones	Costa Rican currency

195

Conquistadores	16th-century Spanish explorers in the New World
Contras	short for 'contrarrevolucionarios' – they opposed the Sandinista revolution
córdobas	Nicaraguan currency
corre!	run!
cuidado	care
descalzo	barefoot
diamante	diamond
diario	daily newspaper; diary
España	Spain
esperanza	hope
evangélicos	Protestants
exoneración	exoneration
gaseosa	a soft drink
gringo	a fair-haired foreigner
guardia	a policeman; the police
hora	hour
iglesia	church
inglés/a	Englishman/woman
isletas	small islands
ladrón	thief
lechuga	lettuce; water weed
linterna	torch
machucar	to beat repeatedly
malecón	seaside or riverside promenade
mañana	tomorrow; or just 'not today'
marginado	someone excluded
mercado	a market
miseria	need, penury
moderno	modern
monte	jungle
muelle	mole, quay
nueva	new
número	number
oriental	eastern
palabra	word

panga	outboard canoe
panguero	a boatman
pato	a duck
paz	peace
pie	foot
plaza	a public square
prensa	the press
refugio	a refuge; lodge
seca	dry
Sendero Luminoso	Shining Path
sinchi	Peruvian commando
somocista	a supporter of the Somoza regime
uno	one
vida	life
villas	towns

Appendix B

Team Members

Hovercraft Expedition Team April–September 1995

Jonathan Allan
Robert Babington-Smith
Sqn Ldr Dick Bell
Alan Blake
Peter Blatchford
Harold Briley, OBE
Scott Carson
Robert Case-Green
David Coates
Sqn Ldr Michael Cole, OBE (Leader)
Nicholas Cole
Matthew Dixon
Wg Cdr Peter Dixon, RAF
Christopher Evans
Jason Evans
Matthew Falkiner
John Green
Sarah Lister
Andrew Mayo
Amanda Miller
Timothy Mitford-Slade
Steve Moody
Iain Morris
Michael Pinkess
Dr Rachel Pinniger
Ken Pollard
Victoria Sinclair
Gareth Smith
Jenny Smith
Brenda Smith
Dennis Smith
Mark Sparrow
Neil Townsend

Hovercraft Expedition 'Student' Team June–September 1995

David Adkins
Philip Adkins
Fg Officer Matthew Brown, RAF
Matthew Elson
Andrew Fishbourne
Alex Helm
Bruce Howard
Jonathan Milne
Robert McGregor
Alex Murray
Flight Lt. Mark Ponting, RAF
Andrew Rose
Jonathan Thomas

Supporters' Visit to Nicaragua May–June 1995

Wg Cdr Stan Baldock, DFM, MBE

198

Appendix B

Richard Blake
Margaret Blake
Kimberly Bruner
Nicholas Case-Green
Josie Case-Green
Jackie Cole
Sally Denyer
Beryl Ferenczy
Kate Harris
Gerry Miller
Margaret Miller
Dorothy Reilly

Supporters' Visit to Nicaragua July 1995

Jenny Cole
Shona Cooper
Robert Cooper
Jamie Russell

Spring STEP Teams in Nicaragua

Nueva Guinea (April–June 1995)
Bluefields (June–August 1995)

David Beard
Julian Cox
Nigel Eady
William Elphinston (Leader)
Christianne Fritz
John Higgs
Hannah Kelland
Catriona Ling
Cindy Parker (Leader)
Nathan Phillingham
Urike Schollhorn
Joy Swain
Lucy Watson

Bluefields (April–June 1995)
Nueva Guinea (June–August 1995)

Louise Ashford
Dale Buckton

John Burwood
Angus Douglas
Mark Fairweather-Tall (Leader)
Fiona Kirkpatrick
David Langmead
James MacDougall
Philippa Masters
Judy Mullins
Laura Prideaux
Elizabeth Vaughan

Follow-up Teams

Scunthorpe Methodist Churches
Building third phase of school at Bluefields

Preparation team
February–March 1996

David Clare
Heather Jordan
Ken Pollard (Leader)
Rosemary Rees
Digby Staley

Summer team
July–August 1996

Elisabeth Adkins
Joanne Adkins
Rev. Lawrence Copley (Leader)
Jenny Cuthbertson
Joy Davies
Richard Digby
Rhianna Fardell
David Gladstone
Peter Maw
Mavis McKeon
Ken Pollard (Leader)
Lilian Pollard
Helen Roberts
Elayna Shenstone
Lisa Smith
David Sellars
Neil Taylor

The Naked Feet of Nicaragua

All Souls, Langham Place, 'Wetfoot'

Kitchen for orphanage at Los Brasiles
July–August 1993

Angela Hayes-Allen
Sibylle Von Bentivegni
Noel Burke
Bridget Carr
Rhiannon Desmond
Chris Ekwonna
Andrea Goodwin
Yvonne Hall
Iain Morris (Leader)
Brenda Muckley (Leader)
Alica Kawoya
Frances Kong
Robert Truesdale
Geoff Tunnicliffe
Joanne Westland
Amanda Whybrow
Christina Yianni

Kitchen for Agricultural Training Centre and Christian Conference facility at Juigalpa
July–September 1996

Alan Bishop
Jo Ann Buckenham
Eleanor Cheetham
Naomi Herbert
David Langmead
Judy Mullins
Jennifer Nunn
Tim Rogers
Ed Russell
Liz Stewart (Leader)

Hovercraft Engineers
July–September 1996

James Gibson
James Macbeath

Appendix C

Project Supporters

Commercial Support

Bowring Aviation Ltd
Body Shop, Gloucester
Beacon Packaging Ltd
Britannia Zinc Ltd
Bally Ltd
British Wax Refining Company
Brittany Ferries
Budget Rent a Car (Nicaragua)
Burmah Castrol (UK)
Bluefields Lumber Co
   (Nicaragua)
BP Oil (UK)
BP Solar International
City and Financial Printing
   Service Ltd
Chivers-Hartley
Continental Airlines
Coffee Man (Walton-on-Thames)
Classic Crystal Water
Distributidora Tropical
   (Nicaragua)
Furmanite Ltd
Griffon Hovercraft
Glass and Glazing Federation
Hapag-Lloyd
Howe Catering
Kraft Jacobs Suchard
KHD-DEUTZ (GB)

Jacksons Building Centres
Kodak (Nicaragua)
Lloyds Bank Plc
Land Rover Plc
La Prensa (Nicaragua)
Legal & General Plc
Minnaar Plc
Maxell (UK) Ltd
Magellan (UK) Ltd
Morgan Automation
J P Morgan
Pepsi-Cola (Nicaragua)
Penderel Press
Pozuelo Foods (Nicaragua)
Redbreast Industrial Equipment
Salt & Dukes Ltd
Shell (Nicaragua)
Swift Cookware
Toyota Rent a Car (Nicaragua)
VW & Honda Car Dealership
   (Nicaragua)
Weatherford UK Ltd
Wickes (DIY)
Wrights (Sandbach) Ltd

Pharmaceutical Supporters (donated essential medicines)

Bayer
Braun Medical

Chauvin
Cusi
Dermal Labs
Duphar
Evans Medical
Glaxo
Lederle Labs
Lilly
Norton Healthcare
Rhone-Poulenc Rorer
Searle
Smith & Nephew
3M

Note
Anti-snake venom was purchased from:

Instituto Clodomiro of
San José, Costa Rica

**Supporters from Trusts/Churches/
Voluntary Organisations**

Aldridge Methodist Church
John Allats Foundation
All Souls, Langham Place
All Saints, Sidmouth
Anderson Trust
Barclay Church Sunday School
Bishops of Oxford's Outreach
  Fund
Bishopstoke Evangelical Church
Bodenham Christian Fellowship
Book Aid
Brownhills & Pelsall Methodist
  Circuit
Burnage Family Church
Chiltern 41 Club
Christ Church, Fulwood
Christchurch, Holmer Green
Civil Service Retirement
  Fellowship
Darleston Trust
Daske Trust

WKH Dyer Trust
Eleven/50 Club, Exeter
Erica Leonard Trust
Gales Youth Trust
Gammadoren Trust
Grace Trust
Gilcomston South Church
Gorsley Baptist Church
Grey Wyrley High School
Hampshire County Council
  Youth Trust
Hirwaun English Methodist
  Church
International Presbyterian
  Church, Liphook
Kensal Evangelical Church
Knowleson Trust
Llantwit Major Baptist Church
Longhope Church
Longport Methodist Church
Leicester West Methodist Circuit
Maidstone Lions Club
Maurice Laing Foundation
Meridan Primary School
Millingtons Charity
Monkton Combe School
Morden Baptist Church
Nailsea Methodist Church
Newport Baptist Church
Nicaraguan Bible Society
Oasis Fellowship, Nailsea
Probus Club of Maidstone
RMCS Chapel
Rotary Club of Banbury
Rotary Club of Cannock
Rotary Club of Newent
Rotary Club of Ross-on-Wye
Rugby National Trust
St Andrews, High Wycombe
St Mawgan Parish Church
St Michael and All Angels,
  Blackheath
St Pauls Church, Banbury
St Saviours, Guildford
Scripture Gift Mission

Sheffield Male Voice Choir
Tallowood Baptist Church,
  Houston, Texas
Union Baptist Church, High
  Wycombe
Upton St Leonards Church,
  Gloucester
Wallington Missionary Auction
Westhill Primary School, Canock
Willshall Association
World Relief
Zion Methodist Church

Individual Supporters
1994–5

Abarca, Eduardo
Abbott, Sqn Ldr Bob & Elma
Alemán, Dr Arnoldo Lacayo
Allan, Rev. Don & Barbara
Baines, David
Baldock, Wg Cdr Stan & Gladys
Barber, Margaret
Barker, Keith & Katrin
Barkey, Maurice
Bennett, Clive & Pauline
Bernard, Martin
Bewley, Rob & Rosie
Black, Brian
Blatchford, Steve & Mary
Bothe, Andrea
Bowring, Carole
Brooks, Wg Cdr David
Brown, H. E. Roger
Bruins, Cor & Audrey
Bruner, George, Novice & Kim
Burton, Dr Tim
Caldera, Milton
Calvert, Raul
Case, Frances
Case-Green, Nick & Josie
Chamorro, Pedro Joaquín
Clare, Colonel Jeremy
Clear, Bill & Shirley
Coates, Michael & Judith

Cole, John & Betty
Cole, Ron & Anne
Colebourne family
Collins, Nigel
Cooper, Roger & Shona
Coronel, Carlos & Jean
Coronel, Ian
Cottingham, Tony & Maureen
Cox, Michael
Craddock family
Craddock, Cynthia
Cross, Edgar
Cubin, Barbara
Culver, H. E. John & Margaret
Davies, Fred
Davies, Rev. Stanley
Day, John & Cressida
Denyer, Sally
Dibdin, Peter
Dinkledein, Margaret
Drew, Dr Donald
Dunlop, Jim & Julia
Dyer, Wilfred
Edmonds, Harold & Peggy
Ellis, Roy & Mary
Emery, Alan
Evans, Richard & Lydia
Ewbank, Lady Joyce
Farrer, Simon & Maureen
Ferenczy, Peter & Fiona
Field, Brian & Sheila
Fifield, Edward & Stella
Foister, Margaret
Ford, Don & Madge
Forshaw, Betty
Foster, Jack & Marion
Gallaugher, Sqn Ldr Paddy &
  Sue
Garrad, Brian & Zena
Gifford, Graham & Geraldine
Gifford, John
Gooch, Keith
Gooderidge, Roger
Goodman, Wg Cdr Gordon &
  Sue

Gould, Lynne
Goulding, Jeff & Sarah
Goulding, Kevin
Green, Marion
Guzmán, Fernando
Hamilton, Lynne
Hannant, Shona
Harley, Robert
Harris, Colin
Hartshorn, Betty
Hayward, Hannah
Head, Viscountess Alicia
Heath, Rt Hon. Sir Edward
Helm, Michael & Christine
Henderson, Dr Alex & Adrienne
Hill, Peter & Janet
Humphrey, Lady Agnes
Irvine, Nick
Jaentschke, Ed & Ligia
James, Garfield & Audrey
James, Lilian
Jarrett-Kerr, Brigadier Alfred
Jonker, Mary
Jordan, Barry & Val
Jordan, Dr Michael & Judith
Juliffe, David
Keene, Philip
Kessel, Heinz
Kessler, Dr John & Margaret
Knapton, Keith & Helena
Kraay, Pieter
Kuhrt, Olive
Lacayo, Roger
Laing, Sir Maurice
Lauder, Angela
Linnecar, Vera
Lister, Mark
Lister, Steve
Lockwood family
Macdonald, John
Mackay, Rev. William & Eva
Mackintosh, Grant
MacQuigg, Claud & Aileen
Mason, Denis
McCormick, Jim & Audrey

McMillan, Alison
Mead, Prof. Denys & Rosemary
Merriman, David & Catherine
Millard, John
Miller, Daisy
Millington, Roy & Helen
Milnes, Rebecca
Mitford-Slade, Major Tony
  & Dawn
Mojet, Huib & Anne
Moore, Gwyneth
Muckley, Brenda
Myers, Barry
Neal, John & Sue
Newborough, Harry & Mary
Nichols, Dr Andrew
Nightingale, Jo & Jill
Nightingale, Phyllis
Ogden, Phyllis
O'Mara, Margaret
Owen, John
Owers, David & Eileen
Pardoe, Beryl
Pearce, Elizabeth
Pearman, Nick
Pearse, Cecil & Kath
Pegler, Miss
Penman, Harold & Mary
Pessarra, Rev. Al
Pickup, Russell
Pike, John & Angela
Pont, Arthur
Pott, Major John & Anna
Preston, Nigel & Wendy
Read, Bob & Pamela
Reason, Nora
Rees, Rosemary
Reilly, Colin & Dorothy
Reyes, Armando
Richardson, Keith
Rivas, Dr Santiago Leclair
Robinson, Sarah
Rodd, Ken & Muriel
Rose family
Rossiter, Lorraine

Sanderson, Kevin
Sansbury, Muriel
Savage, Commander Anthony
Scourfield-Davis, Gwyn
Sharman, Ruth
Shaw, Dawn
Sherington family
Sherman, William
Slattery, Stanley & Irenee
Smith, Gilbert & Connie
Smith, James & June
Smith, Jeremy & Lois
Snelgrove, Pat
Sneller, Andrew & Lucy
Southam, Christine
Southgate, Chris
Sparrow family
St John, David & Elizabeth

Staplehurst, Douglas
Stevenson family
Swindale, Peter & Anne
Terán, Roberto
Tokey family
Towkins, Justin
Townsend family
Trenchard, Ken
Vijil, Pablo
Watson, Michael, MP
Webb, Muriel
Weir, Norman & Jessie
Wetton, David & Clare
White, Richard
Williams, Dr Sarah
Wilson, Mabel
Woolford, Colin & Brenda
Zamorán, Freddy

. . . and very many more who sent donations or helped individual hovercrafters and Steppers to raise the personal support for which each was responsible.

To all these, the authors, Project Leader and team members express their warmest appreciation and thanks.

Appendix D

Completed Community Projects in Nicaragua

Projects which took place 1991–96

1991 Noah's Ark Primary School, Mercado Oriental, Managua City
1992 Hogar de Fe Primary School, Los Brasiles
1992 Skills Workshop Community Centre, Urbaite, Ometepe Island
1993 VERBO agricultural barn, Bluefields
1993 Secondary School classrooms, Urbaite, Ometepe Island
1994 VERBO Primary School (Stage 1), Bluefields
1994 Agricultural and Bible Training Centre (CCBIZ), Nueva Guinea
1994 School classrooms, Merida, Ometepe Island
1995 CCBIZ (Stage 2), Nueva Guinea
1995 VERBO Primary School (Stage 2), Bluefields
1996 Hogar de Fe Orphanage extension, Los Brasiles
1996 Kitchen facility for Agricultural and Conference Centre, Las Lomitas, Juigalpa
1996 VERBO Primary School (Stage 3), Bluefields

Hovercraft Project Infrastructures

1995 Hovercraft garage and store, Bluefields
1995 Hovercraft slipway, San Pancho, Rio San Juan
1995 Community lodge, Greytown

Notes

Chapter 1

1. J. S. Holliday, *The World Rushed In* (Simon & Schuster, 1977), p. 452.
2. ibid., p. 416.
3. David McCullough, *The Path Between the Seas* (American Society of Civil Engineers, 1977), p. 34.
4. The Momotombo volcano appeared on a series issued in 1900.

Chapter 2

1. Michael Cole, *Journey to the Fourth World* (Lion Publishing, 1981).
2. Dick Bell, *To the Source of the Yangtze* (Hodder & Stoughton, 1991).
3. Cecil D. Pearse, *Beyond the Lagoon* (Hodder & Stoughton, 1993).
4. James Burney, *History of the Buccaneers of America* (1816, reprinted 1949).
5. Craig L. Dozier, *Nicaragua's Mosquito Shore* (University of Alabama, Texas, 1985).

Chapter 3

1. Peter Dixon, *Amazon Task Force* (Hodder & Stoughton, 1984).
2. In Latin America, a colloquial nickname (of uncertain etymology) for fair-haired foreigners, especially North Americans.

Chapter 6

1. Quoted by Cristiana Chamorro (the President's daughter), 'Restoring Lost Years in Paradise' (*La Prensa*, 22 October 1991).

The Naked Feet of Nicaragua

2. Richard Gott, 'The Latin Conversion', *Guardian Weekly*, 10 June 1995.
3. Comité Evangélico Pro Ayuda a los Damnificados (The Evangelical Committee for Emergency Relief).

Chapter 7

1. The word is colloquial Spanish for 'fluke', i.e. 'a favourable outcome by chance'.
2. William Agudelo in his essay 'San Juan del Norte'.

Chapter 8

1. Tom Pocock, *Horatio Nelson* (Pimlico, 1978), p. 38.
2. Tom Pocock, *Young Nelson in the Americas* (Collins, 1980).
3. The American Declaration of Independence was signed in 1776.
4. Captain Russell Grenfell, RN, *Horatio Nelson* (Greenwood Press, 1978).
5. The Global Positioning System is a navigational aid which produces an exact fix by recourse to RF emissions, received from no fewer than three satellites.
6. Robert Southey, *Life of Nelson* (Naval Institute Press, ed. 1887).

Chapter 9

1. Jaime Incer, *Nicaragua – Viajes Rutas y Encuentros 1502–1838* (Libro Libre, 1990), pp. 389–90.
2. Authors' own free translation of Darío's

> Hermano, tú que tienes la luz, dame la mía.
> Soy como un ciego. Voy sin rumbo y ando a tientas
> Voy bajo tempestades y tormentas,
> Ciego de ensueño y loco de harmonía.

Chapter 10

1. Pronounced so-len-tee-ná-may.
2. *Comunidades de Base*.
3. An island shared today between Haiti and the Dominican Republic.
4. C1arl Bovallius, 'Viaje por Centro América 1881–3', in Ernesto Cardenal, *El Río San Juan* (Latino Editores, 1993).

208